theatre & environment

Theatre &
Series Editors: Jen Harvie and Dan Rebellato

Published

Joel Anderson: *Theatre & Photography*
Vicky Angelaki: *Theatre & Environment*
Susan Bennett: *Theatre & Museums*
Bill Blake: *Theatre & the Digital*
Marvin Carlson: *Theatre & Islam*
Colette Conroy: *Theatre & the Body*
Emma Cox: *Theatre & Migration*
Jim Davis: *Theatre & Entertainment*
Jill Dolan: *Theatre & Sexuality*
Emine Fişek: *Theatre & Community*
Helen Freshwater: *Theatre & Audience*
Jen Harvie: *Theatre & the City*
Nadine Holdsworth: *Theatre & Nation*
Erin Hurley: *Theatre & Feeling*
Dominic Johnson: *Theatre & the Visual*
Joe Kelleher: *Theatre & Politics*
Ric Knowles: *Theatre & Interculturalism*
Petra Kuppers: *Theatre & Disability*
Yair Lipshitz: *Theatre & Judaism*
Brian Lobel: *Theatre & Cancer*
Patrick Lonergan: *Theatre & Social Media*
Caoimhe McAvinchey: *Theatre & Prison*
Bruce McConachie: *Theatre & Mind*
Lucy Nevitt: *Theatre & Violence*
Helen Nicholson: *Theatre & Education*
Lourdes Orozco: *Theatre & Animals*
Lionel Pilkington: *Theatre & Ireland*
Benjamin Poore: *Theatre & Empire*
Paul Rae: *Theatre & Human Rights*
Alan Read: *Theatre & Law*
Dan Rebellato: *Theatre & Globalization*
Trish Reid: *Theatre & Scotland*
Nicholas Ridout: *Theatre & Ethics*
Jo Robinson: *Theatre & the Rural*
Mark Robson: *Theatre & Death*
Juliet Rufford: *Theatre & Architecture*
Elizabeth Schafer: *Theatre & Christianity*
Rebecca Schneider: *Theatre & History*
Lara Shalson: *Theatre & Protest*
Kim Solga: *Theatre & Feminism*
Konstantinos Thomaidis: *Theatre & Voice*
Fintan Walsh: *Theatre & Therapy*
Eric Weitz: *Theatre & Laughter*
David Wiles: *Theatre & Time*
Harvey Young: *Theatre & Race*
Keren Zaiontz: *Theatre & Festivals*

theatre & environment

Vicky Angelaki

BLOOMSBURY
NEW DELHI • LONDON • OXFORD • NEW YORK • SYDNEY

BLOOMSBURY INDIA
Bloomsbury Publishing India Pvt. Ltd
Second Floor, LSC Building No. 4, DDA Complex, Pocket C–6&7,
Vasant Kunj, New Delhi 110070

BLOOMSBURY, BLOOMSBURY ACADEMIC INDIA and the Diana logo are trademarks of Bloomsbury Publishing Plc

First published in India 2025
First published 2019 by RED GLOBE PRESS

This edition published with permission from Bloomsbury Publishing Plc,
50 Bedford Square, London, WC1B3DP, UK

A catalogue record for this book is available from the British Library.
A catalog record for this book is available from the Library of Congress.

ISBN: 978-93-61318-61-0

Printed and bound in India by Replika Press Pvt. Ltd.
To find out more about our authors and books
visit www.bloomsbury.com and sign up for our newsletters

For my grandfather Manolis,
for our walks by the sea.

contents

series editors' preface

The theatre is everywhere, from entertainment districts to the fringes, from the rituals of government to the ceremony of the courtroom, from the spectacle of the sporting arena to the theatres of war. Across these many forms stretches a theatrical continuum through which cultures both assert and question themselves.

Theatre has been around for thousands of years, and the ways we study it have changed decisively. It's no longer enough to limit our attention to the canon of Western dramatic literature. Theatre has taken its place within a broad spectrum of performance, connecting it with the wider forces of ritual and revolt that thread through so many spheres of human culture. In turn, this has helped make connections across disciplines; over the past fifty years, theatre and performance have been deployed as key metaphors and practices with which to rethink gender, economics, war, language, the fine arts, culture and one's sense of self.

Theatre & is a long series of short books which hopes to capture the restless interdisciplinary energy of theatre and performance. Each book explores connections between theatre and some aspect of the wider world, asking how the theatre might illuminate the world and how the world might illuminate the theatre. Each book is written by a leading theatre scholar and represents the cutting edge of critical thinking in the discipline.

We have been mindful, however, that the philosophical and theoretical complexity of much contemporary academic writing can act as a barrier to a wider readership. A key aim for these books is that they should all be readable in one sitting by anyone with a curiosity about the subject. The books are challenging, pugnacious, visionary sometimes and, above all, clear. We hope you enjoy them.

Jen Harvie and Dan Rebellato

foreword by Ian Fairchild

The word 'atmosphere' provides a natural bridge between the theatre and the domain of environmental sciences. Aside from the emotional realm, performances may conjure literal or metaphorical images such as bracing clean air, fetid dungeons and Cowardesque smoke-filled drawing rooms. The scientist invests effort by different means – obtaining information by measurements and modelling – and making predictions. It was through the International Geophysical Year in 1957 that long-term programmes of systematic monitoring of the atmosphere were established. They soon demonstrated a steady upwards creep in the level of carbon dioxide, modulated by a seasonal dip (caused by northern hemisphere photosynthesis) that has been poetically likened to the planet breathing. These rising levels are undetectable to the human senses, but they have a profound effect on heat retention of the air. This, coupled with the impacts of pollution and examination of human activity at the expense of natural ecosystems, has led us to the current environmental crisis. Will Steffen's term 'The Great Acceleration'[1] describes the unprecedented worldwide changes since the middle of the twentieth century. This characterises the Anthropocene, the proposed name for an epoch in which the global impacts of humans on the planet are manifest.

I am grateful to Vicky Angelaki for giving me the opportunity, in the context of a conference at Birmingham in 2016, to develop ideas for outreach about the science of the Anthropocene in a performance context. *Introducing the Anthropocene* has had several outings over the last two years and has informed and provoked audiences (some of whom are participants) in encouraging ways. Scientists bewildered by the commonplace rubbishing of their facts can strike back by embracing the arts to their mutual benefit and especially that of the public.

Ian Fairchild
Emeritus Professor, School of Geography, Earth and Environmental Sciences, University of Birmingham

[1] For more details, see Steffen, Will, et al.. 'The Trajectory of the Anthropocene: The Great Acceleration'. The Anthropocene Review, no. 2, 2015, pp. 81–98.

theatre & environment

In April 2018, I visited Vienna's Kunsthistorisches Museum. I have been there frequently through the years, but this time the space was newly defamiliarised by the temporary exhibition *The Last Day*, consisting of Helmut Wimmer's photography and Karlheinz Essl's sound installation. The sound emulated the natural phenomena encountered in the photographs: crashing waves, strong wind, trees surrendering to its force. Twelve large images depicted various landmark spaces of the museum, except dramatically different. Eerily, in all the photographs, the artworks were still present, witnessing a new moment in history. In some cases, tourists could still be seen enjoying their visit, gazing at the centuries-old masterpieces. Yet, strangely, there were no longer limits between the human-made art, or the space that accommodates it, and nature. In fact, nature had invaded, forcing the point of how much longer we can afford to be complacent, or how much longer those so admired artistic and architectural structures, resilient and enduring through times of conflict, war and destruction, might be able to survive. What if the beautifully landscaped Maria-Theresien-Platz, extending from the Kunsthistorisches to the Naturhistorisches Museum, became a jungle? What if debris suddenly exploded everywhere, the Roman statues now resting on a surface of scattered leaves and fallen branches? What if large mountainous formations suddenly broke through the walls of the Renaissance halls or perhaps lakes and bushes covered the parquet floors? What if wildlife creatures roamed the corridors with the same ease as the affluent tourists? What if the wild sea crashed against the masterful testimonials to all of humanity's histories and grand achievements, the visitors' feet steeped in water? And what if that remarkable marble staircase, where one first pauses to take it all in upon encountering the museum, were covered in snow and ice? Would the imposing statue by Antonio Canova, depicting Theseus as he prevails over the centaur, a symbol of human victory and survival towering over the landing, still be so awe-inspiring? There was no solace in Wimmer and Essl's installation, nor should there be. It provided, to a wide, international audience, a spectatorial base of means and responsibility, a staggering vehicle for the visual realisation of how much was at stake in that very moment. The museum had made it into the twenty-first century to perform a scenario of its own dystopian future, staged more self-reflectively than ever before, asking how much time might still be left.

When it comes to the environment, as well as to many aspects of our social and political experience, our current historical moment feels unprecedented. The 2015

United Nations Climate Change Conference in Paris (30 November–12 December) offered both a crucial forum for reflection and a renewed opportunity for urgent and collective action towards managing the most pressing global crisis of the twenty-first century. Involving all the major players and leading economies with pivotal influence on the handling of this crisis, the conference produced the Paris Agreement, which became available to signatories on 22 April 2016. As we now know, 2016 proved to be a landmark year in terms of political developments received by many as substantial hindrances on the path to international collaboration, not least because some of these developments concerned two leading global powers: the United Kingdom and the United States. In June 2016, the result of the British referendum concerning the country's future within the European Union was announced as favouring the Leave campaign that had supported Brexit with a marginal majority of 52% of the vote. Given the European Union's pivotal role in the Paris conference, as well as in UN action against climate change more broadly, the blow to confidence was significant. In November 2016, the United States experienced a political moment held by some as its Brexit equivalent in terms of its unpredictability and the uncertainty it produced: the election of Donald J. Trump as the country's 45th president. In June 2017, the Trump Administration announced that it would be withdrawing from the Paris Agreement.

Una Chaudhuri, leading scholar in the field of performance and environment, has noted in her work the significance of the present moment, recognising that the policy changes of the Trump administration have necessitated bolder action in solidarity (Climate Lens). Identifying the term 'post-national' as a suitable determiner, unifying rather than dismissive, Chaudhuri frames the unique urgency of the present as transcending local contexts to create a universal call to action (Climate Lens). The term 'post-nation' that she proposes denotes an internationalist community rather than globalised disassociation (Climate Lens). Instead of tying environmental protection to national imperatives or to financial, partisan or even noble governmental concerns, this work clarifies why it ought to be framed as appealing profoundly to our ethical commitment as citizens of our world. The call of Chaudhuri's research group, which identifies as CLIMATE LENS, to apply a syllogism similar to the one that established gender as the ultimate conditioning factor for feminism, making it into a movement, to the climate as focusing angle for all concerns is apt and indicative, reflecting the extent to which the cause ought to be adopted on a humanitarian level (Climate Lens). For Chaudhuri and her research/practitioner activist group, the significance of this refocusing of the question links to reversing hegemonic attitudes of locating human interests at the heart of the environmental issue. The benefit of such a behavioural shift would be the democratising and universalising of the question, stepping away from the dominant conditioning lens of our self-preservational and utilitarian perception of nature. As feminism became a powerful tool for textual and performance analysis, so too, Chaudhuri proposes, can climate become a guide for our future critical discourses, for contemporary theatre production and for revisionist approaches to the canon (Climate Lens).

Any conversation concerning the environment is always equally geared towards the past, present and future. While it is certainly a matter of understanding and accounting for our past transgressions against the planet, performance made and witnessed through the environmental lens seeks to discover how we might begin to adjust our attitudes and implement a shift, not arbitrarily or momentarily but in depth of time and substantive enough to produce future improvement. In the following chapters, this short book discusses representative examples of environmentally aware performance. In so doing, it hopes to draw on paradigms that will provide the reader with a frame of reference specific and yet broad enough to draw conclusions on how our sense of responsibility towards the environment has been handled by artists and theatre-makers in our time.

The Anthropocene and the Eco-lexicon

Few terms have emerged as strongly in the contemporary lexicon as the 'Anthropocene', understood as the time period in which human impact has grown to such an extent that it has caused permanent and lasting consequences for our natural world. Reaching a consensus regarding the precise beginning of the Anthropocene is not a straightforward proposition, due to the range of evidence and the implications – social, political and scientific – of such an acknowledgement. In 2016, the Working Group on the Anthropocene (WGA) underlined its findings by recommending that the era should become officially 'declared' (Carrington). Scientists contributing to the WGA had previously made the compelling argument that in order to account for the Anthropocene, we need to appreciate its historical depth (Zalasiewicz et al. 197), which reaches further into the past than we might imagine given the relatively recent surge in the usage of the term, located in the early 2000s (Zalasiewicz et al. 197). The WGA note that an understanding of the term's origins does not equal a by-default formalisation of the Anthropocene (Zalasiewicz et al. 197), but that its recognition, on the basis of the 'substantial' 'anthropogenic acceleration of processes of erosion and sedimentation' and the 'geological novelty of many human-driven processes', is important (Zalasiewicz et al. 197). The WGA present the options for the starting points of the Anthropocene, identifying pivotal moments whereby, simply put, a differing approach of the individual's relationship to land, as well as technology-accelerating inventions and population growth, could have marked a beginning (Zalasiewicz et al. 198). A consideration of variables leads the authors to propose:

> that the Anthropocene (formal or informal) be defined to begin historically at the moment of detonation of the Trinity A-bomb at Alamogordo, New Mexico, at 05:29:21 Mountain War Time. (± 2 s) July 16, 1945 (1⁄4 11:29:21 Co-ordinated Universal Time 1⁄4 Greenwich Mean Time).
>
> (Zalasiewicz et al. 200)

Long before 'Anthropocene' became a term, a host of other related terms had been appearing, revealing a turn towards heightened environmental awareness. From early instances to more recent ones, we may be surprised to find that some of the terminology is first encountered further into the past than we might expect. For all of the examples that follow on this page and ensuing pages for the etymology of words, my research source is the *Oxford English Dictionary* (*OED*). From 'ecologic' (1894), 'ecologist' (1893), 'ecological' (1879) and the oldest form, 'ecology' (1875), environmental vocabulary, sometimes in the plural rather than singular form provided here, branched out in combination forms with the prefix 'eco-' (occasionally not hyphenated), which begins to enter discourse more widely in the early twentieth century. Within this lexicon, terms range from scientific, academic and observational descriptors objectively denoting social developments to terms that, if not colloquial, carry derogatory or even mocking and insulting connotations. Examples in the former category include 'ecogeographical' (1939), 'eco-cultural' (1949), 'ecospace' (1969), 'eco-consciousness' (1971) and 'eco-awareness' (1973), or 'eco-city' (1973), 'eco-catastrophe' (1969), 'eco-crisis' (1970), 'eco-damage' (1977) and even 'eco-tragedy' (1992), along with numerous other composites. Instances in the latter group feature 'eco-freak' (1969), 'eco-nut' (1971), 'ecodoomster' (1972), 'eco-fashionable' (1974), 'ecofascism' (1983), 'eco-warrior' (1987), 'eco-babble' (1989), 'eco-craz[y]' (1990), 'eco-hip' (1991), 'eco-smugness' (1992) or even 'eco-twats' (1996). Also recently, an appropriation of the form linked to a widespread, occasionally fashionable though not necessarily devoid of substance engagement with environmental issues, coinciding with globalisation and the recognition of climate change as a major threat, has also appeared, producing, indicatively, terms such as 'eco-audit' (1980), 'ecotourism' (1982), 'eco-label' (1989), 'eco-tax' (1990), 'eco-architect' (1991), 'eco-efficiency' (1992), 'eco-literacy' (1993), 'eco-charities' (2000), 'eco-friendly' (2000), 'eco-footprint' (2002), 'eco-advocacy' (2003), 'eco-gastronomic' (2004) and 'eco-protester' (2007). All of the above underline human agency in the fate of the environment. At the same time, the growing engagement of the arts with the environment has produced terms intermixing 'eco-' with different performance and visual arts genres, stretching back to 1970, when 'eco-art' makes its first appearance. The environment, of course, is not only a social but also a political issue, as the fervour of the terms attacking ecological activity also indicates. Words like 'ecopolitics' (1944), 'ecomanagement' (1968), 'eco-justice' (1973), 'eco-raider' (1973) or 'eco-terrorism' ((1980), indicating either opposing side on the spectrum of meanings for the term), as well as 'ecofeminism' (1980) and 'eco-socialism' (1985) are representative examples.

Towards an Eco-theatre and Eco-performance

To date, notable efforts that have addressed, in various ways, concerns of ecology, environment, climate and nature (terms not to be conflated, though frequently interchangeable) in the context of performance, have included *On Ecology*, the special issue of *Performance Research: A Journal of the Performing Arts* (17.4), and *Environmentalism*, the themed issue of *Research in Drama Education: The Journal of Applied Theatre and Performance* (17.2) (both 2012). It was in that same year that *Readings in Performance and Ecology*, edited by Wendy Arons and Theresa J. May, scholars whose impact on the field has been consistent and considerable, was also published. In 2015, the journal for the Center for Sustainable Practice in the Arts, *CSPA Quarterly*, published its *On Environment* volume, which included reflections on performance. A year later, a special issue of *Green Letters: Studies in Ecocriticism*, guest edited by Carl Lavery, focused on the theme of *Performance and Ecology* and asked *What Can the Theatre Do*? The Routledge volume of the material in the form of an edited collection followed in 2018.

The field has continued to flourish, with publications probing the issue of performance and climate change from different specialist angles and gaining from the growing interest in the relationship between theatre and science more broadly. Moreover, research forums such as the Performance and Ecology Working Group of ASTR (American Society for Theatre Research) provide a basis for ongoing dialogue. Other initiatives have included the Culture & Ecology Network, a forum for academics and practitioners (which, like the ASTR group features the work of Lisa Woynarski), and Julie's Bicycle, a charity committed to sustainability and fostering change within creative practice towards an intervention in working methods and thematic focus that might materialise on the artistic and the audience fronts. There had been significant antecedents, prominent among them the journal *Interdisciplinary Studies in Literature and Environment* (since 1993); *Nature Performed: Environment, Culture and Performance*, edited by Bronislaw Szerszynski, Wallace Heim and Claire Waterton (2003); Gabriella Giannachi and Nigel Stewart's edited collection *Performing Nature: Explorations in Ecology and the Arts* (2006); Baz Kershaw's *Theatre Ecology: Environments and Performance Events* (2007); and Downing Cless's *Ecology and Environment in European Drama* (2010). This list is not intended to be exhaustive but rather to provide the reader with an indication of the timelines and directions in the field in the recent period and until today.

First, this book opens with playwriting, concentrating on work that displays a clear focus on negative human intervention on nature, energy/resource overconsumption/exhaustion/compromise and overpopulation. I discuss how the burgeoning crisis we have been facing has provided the impetus for writing that has often defied social realism to produce new forms and nuanced texts with an environmental pivot. Such explorations have established new directions in the relationship between playwriting and science – which in itself stretches back to the definitive texts of naturalism – and created new strands for what we might describe as socio-environmental and political writing for the stage. Second, I examine the work of directors and companies who have prioritised the environment as a concern. I discuss that this has meant implementing the environmental turn in performance to shape new methods for staging and develop new conditions for spectating, imagining theatre audiences as communities and attacking neoliberalist insularity by promoting stronger civic awareness. Such practice has often also helped redefine the use of institutional spaces and transcend their structural limitations. In turn, this has heightened the feeling of reciprocity among audience/community members by highlighting our shared ethics, responsibilities and mutual implications, attacking passivity and inaction. Third, I consider cross-genre initiatives, taking a broader approach to the definition of theatre and performance. This involves practices that frequently occur beyond institutional spaces to include public installations, platform discussions, interactive and participatory performance events, sustainability think tanks in theatre-making and collective projects that enable a performance of ethically driven citizenship.

Playwriting

Although the environment has yet to take hold as a consistent reference and framing angle in the work of contemporary playwrights in the way that other major social and political issues have, most notably the economy and critiques of capitalism, concerns of climate change have featured in significant texts of the recent period in various iterations. This book concentrates predominantly on new plays, yet it is relevant to the grounding of this discussion to note the enduring attention that one of the most impactful texts to explore the concern of environment, economy and community across theatre history has been receiving from theatres, companies and audiences alike. The play is Henrik Ibsen's *An Enemy of the People* (1882), which transcends local contexts and cultural specificity. The plot is as follows: the protagonist, Dr. Thomas Stockmann, establishes that the town baths are contaminated and feels compelled to divulge this information to his community. While others in positions of power and authority, from the mayor (Dr. Stockmann's brother) to the journalists at the local paper, ultimately position themselves against informing their fellow citizens, Dr. Stockmann remains committed to his decision and to transparency. When he shares his knowledge in a meeting with his community, the results run against his expectations. Dr. Stockmann emphasises morals and responsibility, but his words are interpreted as criticism. He becomes alienated from his peers, now a mass turning against him. As Dr. Stockmann becomes an outcast in the town that he attempted to protect, the title of Ibsen's play echoes. This title of course also creates ambiguity as to who the enemy of the people actually is, on what terms this is defined and how any public might become vulnerable to demagogy.

Through Dr. Stockmann's story, Ibsen put to his audience questions regarding political authority and ethics, as well as the role of the expert, within a civic community that needs to be alerted and also to adapt to the realities of an imminent health threat. In recent years, high-profile productions have appeared in major international stages. At the Schaubühne Berlin, director Thomas Ostermeier and dramaturg Florian Borchmeyer returned to the play in 2012 for an updated version that has subsequently toured extensively. In 2013, playwright David Harrower and director Richard Jones brought their version to London's Young Vic. In 2017, a version by writer/

director Frank-Patrick Steckel, director Jette Steckel and dramaturg Anika Steinhoff opened at Vienna's Burgtheater. According to the data held by the National Library of Norway concerning the international productions of Ibsen plays until 2014, *An Enemy of the People* was staged from 2000 onwards in 234 different productions ('Alt om Henrik Ibsen').

The Burgtheater show directed by Steckel and designed by Florian Lösche with costumes by Sibylle Wallum visibly marks Dr. Stockmann as both scientist and outsider from the beginning. Semiotically, the two signs come to merge: expert equals outcast. Dr. Stockmann wears an oversized orange parka, carrying his orange metal durability briefcase, never too far from him throughout the duration of performance – both become visual trademarks in this production. However supported Stockmann may be by his family, here too, as in Ibsen's source text, his journey is, ultimately, a solitary one, set to his own moral compass. The visual connotations of Stockmann's costume are such that we might imagine him on an expedition in Antarctica, for example, but he is instead making his way across the hometown, where everyone else seems blissfully immersed in their ignorance. At one point, in the final stretch of the show, Stockmann (Joachim Meyerhoff), now at one with the community of spectators, turns his back on the stage, shunned by his own community. He trespasses in the space of the audience, where he installs himself in one of the auditorium chairs, delivering an indignant monologue and wrapping his orange parka around him like a shield, protected in the power that the truth of his knowledge affords him.

The monologue prompts direct communication with the audience, rendering Ibsen's interventionist play as urgent today as when it was first performed. Spectators double up as Stockmann's community, both real, in the space of performance, and a physical extension of the withdrawn, non-receptive fictional community on the stage; they have the option and power of intervention, dialogue and response. They can do better. In the Burgtheater, the rigidity and apathy of Stockmann's onstage community was aptly captured in their representation in the shape not of humans but of giant gnomes, crossing the stage in their staunch physical mass to isolate and eventually push out and ostracise Stockmann, who is literally dispensed with, removed from the edge of town, dropped off the stage. Such is the potency of language in Stockmann's pleas throughout the play and especially in the confrontation scene with his community and the one that follows with the audience that when Steckel closes the piece with Zaza Rusadze's striking video art, this feels neither extrinsic nor instructive. On the contrary, it provides us with a pause, a moment for taking stock, the opportunity for shared reflection.

The video, which runs for minutes rather than moments, stretching across a giant screen that covers the perimeter of the Burgtheater stage, plays to the sound of Radiohead's 'No Surprises' and offers a public indictment of media, communities, political authorities and, above all, complacency – of observation and inaction, or insufficient intervention. It begins with the image of a surfer negotiating an overwhelming wave in slow motion. The image forms a staple reference throughout as shots of a news anchor in a television studio and of different events depicting large-scale damage, environmental catastrophe and extreme shifts linked to climate change play out in front of the audience to a tune of prevailing calm and quiet over any distress or struggle – literally captured by, if not juxtaposed with, the Radiohead song. The activism of the play and video, the latter reminiscent of the aesthetics of environmental preservation organisations, are neither artificially transposed nor indulgently incidental. On the contrary, Steckel's aesthetics speak to a broader philosophy, revealed not only in the choice of play but also in the fact that the director had spent time working for Greenpeace. Steckel speaks resolutely on collective responsibility and the thematic durability of Ibsen's play, a metaphor for resilience in itself, but also makes it clear that, in the current moment especially, an intervention on the text that takes a resolute approach to Stockmann's character and establishes him as an activist driven by principle is essential (Petsch). Steckel also emphasises that her production is built on the conviction that Stockmann is on the right side of the dispute (Petsch). The contemporary resonance of the play as underlined by Steckel removes this production from any kind of facile opportunism and brings it into performance activism. As she notes, the environmental question did not require much in the way of dramaturgical mediation to be rendered relevant. 'The topic is unfortunately more virulent than ever', she observes (Petsch).[1]

[1] In German, 'das Thema ist leider virulenter denn je'.

However incontestable its urgency, presenting Ibsen's play in a production that not only avoids the risk of making it appear pedantic or didactic but also delivers it on the stage as fresh as a piece of new writing is significant. In her discourse, Steckel emerges as no less committed to environmental preservation than is Katie Mitchell, whose work is discussed in the following section. Regarding individual levels of agency, Steckel notes that, unfortunately, humans are not realising that we need to be making the most of the time available to each of us to combat climate change, leading to the issue acquiring dramatic dimensions (Petsch). This is very much the perspective that Ibsen's *An Enemy of the People/Ein Volksfeind* delivered at the Burgtheater in a production that began in late 2017 and would remain in repertoire, as per the model typically followed in German-speaking Europe, thereby offering a continuing vehicle for the exploration of the issue rather than concentrated action over a shorter period of time and creating a significant afterlife for the play itself.

Science, morals and ethics as seeds for experimentation have of course been visible in new plays too, not least Ella Hickson's *Oil* (Almeida Theatre, director Carrie Cracknell), which in 2016 reinforced the link between naturalism and environmentalism in contemporary playwriting. Through its focus on human nature alongside science and industry, the text also tugged at the archetypal strings of family and predisposition. *Oil* was different from how contemporary playwrights had predominantly engaged with climate change until that point. It did not use the minimalist forms of Duncan Macmillan, as in *Lungs* (2011), for example, nor did it produce large-scale protest pieces like Mike Bartlett's, most notably *Earthquakes in London* (2010).[2] And while both Macmillan and Bartlett use the couple, or the family unit, as the anchor for greater crisis, Hickson went a step further by paying specific attention to female lineage. As women, through childbearing, create the future of humanity, so too are they the agent for its destruction. Hickson traces the journey of a woman, in different versions and iterations of herself, through time, conceptualising her as mother, entrepreneur, ambitious individual and eventually a jaded, desensitised entity who has given up on her agency. The key figure of the mother is May, although her daughter Amy is also a significant protagonist and grounding device as she experiences her own journey. The play ends in a dystopian projection of the future, with mother and daughter destroyed by their insularity, excluded from developments and divorced from society, offering a meaningful attack on neoliberalism. We cannot call *Oil* a purely formally experimental play, nor can we describe it as fully realist. The indeterminacy far from reduces its significance, which rests in how the play applies naturalist formulas to concerns of female social involvement, dismantling the binary of the Madonna/whore and establishing the female figure at the heart of developments that may have sought to improve

[2] For an extensive discussion of both plays as texts and in production, see Angelaki, Vicky. *Social and Political Theatre in 21st-Century Britain: Staging Crisis*. Bloomsbury, 2017.

quality of life and democratise resources but that eventually led to the saturation, the monetisation and, ultimately, the obsolescence of nature.

Like most plays that deal with transgressions against the environment, land and/or resources, *Oil* deals with transgressions between humans. Hickson traces these in different tableaux unfolding against varying social, political and historical backdrops, although May remains a permanent fixture. So does, from a certain point onwards, Amy. The child, later seen in older ages, including as an adult, is first mentioned as a foetus in the opening scene, which shows us May as a pregnant worker on a remote Cornwall farm in 1889, living in harsh conditions. We then see May as a young mother with a small child (1908); a middle-aged mother with a teenager (1970) and young adult daughter (2021); and an aged mother and middle-aged daughter in the post-apocalyptic finale. The final scene takes place on the same farm as in the beginning, but we are now in 2051. Through the image of farmers living in extreme poverty, as we witness at the start, Hickson shows us the antagonism of human and nature but also the individual who strives for a better life and to whom new resources, such as an oil lamp and all that this means for other uses of the valuable commodity, are alluring and essential. From the beginning of *Oil*, the survival of nature is set in stark contrast to human survival, and the primal instincts of a mother-to-be provide the catalytic force for the pursuit of better material conditions. The formal structure of Hickson's play, as the past gives birth to the future, mirrors the impending birth we hear about in the play's first scene. The anagrammatic link between the names of the two protagonists – May and Amy – is not only a reference to the mother-daughter relationship, but also to cause and effect, genealogies of ambition and repercussion and past and future being interlocked in a process of constant rebirth and regression, as the world folds back into itself, with mistakes repeated despite occasionally noble intentions, and lessons not learned. Transgressions against nature are always destined to be repeated to the point of ultimate exhaustion, each time under new pretexts, the play suggests.

That the play closes back where it opened is testament to Hickson's caustic take on the problematic past-future and ignorance-knowledge binaries. Despite more information and resources, actual illumination has failed to materialise, as *Oil* renders evident, in an ironic nod to one of its most potent images, the mesmerised farmers gazing at the oil lamp, which has delivered them from darkness, in the beginning. The grotesque image of the complacent, withdrawn, isolated and insulated (literally, in so-called fat suits) mother and daughter that we witness at the end of the play offers satire rather than high drama. It suits a text that never quite sides with its characters despite recognising and even empathising with their dilemmas and predicaments. Ultimately, by investing in the female and maternal and accentuating it throughout, *Oil* asks its women, who are always agents and never passive, until inactions of their own and of previous generations render them so, to step outside their individual frames of reference and view the bigger picture. That they fail to do so offers substantially more than a depiction of the tribulations in mother-daughter relationships: it captures that as the duo repeats itself, so does everything else. Therefore, loops, like vicious circles of choices and attitudes, are far from easy to challenge, let alone break. It is not an optimistic take on humanity's agency in the environmental crisis, but it was an apt one in the autumn of 2016, as both the United Kingdom and the United States of America began to fold back into isolationist trends, which, among other shifts of focus, also implied their desire for limited regulation and prioritisation of their own interests, framed nationally and internationally.

Whereas naturalism certainly offers a suitable framework for environmental crisis, so does abstraction. No other contemporary British play, perhaps, has captured the relationship between neoliberalism, capitalism, the environment, globalisation and formal experimentation more aptly than Caryl Churchill's *Far Away* (2000). It is a text so prescient that it still startles because of the departure towards profound revisions in the relationship between drama and politics. Even before 2000, and particularly the second decade of the twenty-first century, when alternative forms infiltrated the norm, displacing social realism as the dominant playwriting narrative, we had been witnessing signs of a new politicised aesthetics of experimentation. This was especially notable, other than in the theatre of Caryl Churchill, in the late work of Harold Pinter and in the plays of Martin Crimp and of Sarah Kane. *Far Away* delivered a decisive shift at the turn of the new century: from fractured families, political oppression and labour exploitation, it opened up to war, persecution and environmental catastrophe while pushing formal innovation forward. It picked up concerns that Churchill had already begun exploring in earlier work, including the remarkable *Not Not Not Not Not Enough Oxygen* (1971), which anticipated the suffocating urban conditions of the then-distant future in 2010.

More recently, as humanity has been making its way deeper into the second decade of the new century, conditions have been more than ripe for what we might describe as a companion piece. This arrived in the shape of Churchill's play *Escaped Alone* (early 2016), which, like *Far Away*, preceded yet sensed the tectonic shifts that the watershed year 2016 would produce for humanity (the vote for Brexit; the vote for Trump; the growing concern over toxic masculinities), followed by the unravelling of actions in 2017 (the US retreat from the Paris Agreement and the exposure of widespread abusive institutionalised structures against women rank among the most significant ones). Where *Far Away*, through the lens of one family's perspective, reveals a world where events have escalated and nature too has become weaponised and turned hostile agent, as a radical account of the economised, for-profit, political, gain-driven, neo-militant world, *Escaped Alone* uses women's experiences as a filter through which global catastrophe, extensive dissipation and absolute disintegration are processed. Churchill does not show; she tells. The apocalypse is communicated through the characters' descriptions and not through literal representation. As in *Far Away*, so in *Escaped Alone* are there multiple levels of reference, and although it is never staged, the degree of saturation is no less dramatic than in plays that depict such nightmarescapes literally, an example of which I discuss later in this section. *Escaped Alone* parallels two primary fields of abuse: one is society's systemic mistreatment of women; the other is its systematic exploitation of resources. The common denominator for both actions is unaccountability. In *Escaped Alone*, Churchill reveals the moment when the world must be confronted and catch up with consequences: the trauma now becomes collective, as the world has been drained, like the women have been discarded. Despite its progress, or perhaps because of it, society has now reverted to extreme levels of primal survival. As with *Far Away*, *Escaped Alone* is not a by-default climate change play that declares itself as such. This is also where the major power of these plays lies. They rely on what we might have once described as allusion, but given the cataclysmic shifts in the natural and political landscape, it might now be more aptly understood as poetic licence on account of a not altogether unimaginable future, however remote for current generations.

Escaped Alone is still relatively early in its production journey, but *Far Away* has enjoyed a trajectory extensive enough for the play to enter a new phase in its history with productions that use the promenade, site-specific staging methods more commonly associated with companies that produce devised performance. In the summer of 2017, the company Corcadorca produced precisely such an interpretation on Spike Island, Co. Cork. For this show, spectators had to journey to Cobh to board a ferry that would in turn transfer them to the performance site. The overall experience would last slightly over two hours, including the ferry ride, which is indicative of the play's short duration. Home to Fort Mitchel, the disused barracks, Spike Island once served as a military base. Its remoteness and yet relative proximity to land meant that the location echoed the equally literal and ironic meaning of Churchill's title: this was both an isolated locale and one that is closer than we might think, never too far removed in the past that we might forget that histories of conflict move cyclically. The staging, therefore, offered an embodied parable.

As performance space, Spike Island comes with a loaded history. Having begun as a monastic settlement in the seventh century, in later stages it was not only the site of different prisons, including the Fort Mitchel prison, operational from 1985 to 2004 (and therefore still active in the first years after Churchill's play was written; other sources cite the date of closure as 2005, see O'Riordan), but also the site of violent incidents, off limits to visitors prior to its recent emergence as a tourist attraction (O'Riordan, Roseingrave). In 1985, a serious riot erupted on the island when prisoners gained control. This is an event that, if part of the spectators' shared cultural memory, when considered alongside the apocalyptic imagery of Churchill's text and the ferociousness of land engendering uncertain outcomes as described within it, could dramatically enhance the sense of uncertainty emanating from the play. In the eerie context of attending a performance with themes of persecution and precariousness on an island, more exposed to external conditions than in most shows, uncertainty stems from both nature and politics. In any case, the two are intrinsically interwoven. As Patrick Lonergan observes in his reflection on Corcadorca's production, all sensations emerging from the production landscape – from the travel experience by sea to the shift from day to night, the change in temperature and the fact that this is a natural setting rather than a theatre – play an important part. Nature and its creatures that we hear about especially in the closing section of the play, Lonergan adds, are never far from us as spectators, which intensifies our experience. At the same time, we are mindful that even though we might feel separated from it because of the distance from land, the world is never far away, and technology will always intrude: 'a light that you might think is a planet slowly becoming visible in the night sky turns out to be the late flight into Cork Airport from Heathrow, for example' (Lonergan).

Lonergan's commentary captures the feel of the performance, expressing how the play revolves around two poles: oligarchic violence and resource drain. The latter is a theme that *Far Away* explores not only from the primary angle of the destruction of nature but also from the aspect of the consumption of humans as resources themselves, deployed to serve capitalist and militant purposes and ultimately exhausted as brutally as nature has been. After all, here, nature has also been rendered militant and commandeered for political purpose. Faced with a play that deals with imprisonment and disposability, attendees of the Spike Island production would find it difficult to ignore the historical significance of the location, which includes facts such as high mortality rates and human rights violations while in custody (Kelleher) – a theme echoing in Churchill's play. Then there is the question of a different kind of autonomy on Spike Island: the place is a biotope unto itself, producing powerful interference with our spectatorial frames of perception, stemming from the island's last remaining inhabitants: creatures of nature.

Lonergan's references to wind turbines in the distance, a form of human agency deployed in technology towards a collaboration with nature, or the Heathrow flight, another form of human agency deployed to serve mobility needs that burden nature, are also poignant. Flight paths and airports as interventions on – or better, interferences with – urban ecologies and cause for alteration in communities' ways of life, whether we take this to mean convenience or a depleted environment, are central themes in another play that, like *Far Away*, brings climate change to the table as part of an array of other themes: Simon Stephens's *Wastwater* (2011). Here, action is located in the vicinity of Heathrow Airport, and the play repeatedly refers to and engages with the airport as it unfolds. It is equally difficult to describe *Far Away* and *Wastwater* as exclusively climate change plays. The significance of both texts lies in their ability to place natural disaster as part of a much more complex web of intrigue and to demonstrate it for what it is: a product of human desire for control and domination, lack of precautions and our inability to either view ourselves as part of the problem or to distance ourselves from it enough for objective judgement so that collective action on a global scale can progress.[3]

Corcadorca's staging intervention on *Far Away* contributes to ongoing dialogues regarding the flexibility of plays and the ways in which text might enter a dynamic relationship with the performance space. A setting like Spike Island enables the hues in Churchill's text to take shape and, beyond verbal imagery, to acquire a tangible quality that, at the same time, far from compromises the poetry in *Far Away*. In fact, the landscape embodies the vastness of form and content, rendering the audience part of it, sharing in an experience. That this experience helps assert *Far Away*, close to 20 years since its premiere, as an Anthropocene play, as Lonergan also notes, makes for an even richer end result. For meaningful revivals, or indeed for new plays that take on the challenge of climate change, we need to think as ambitiously about a venue as the plays themselves think about the topic they take on. Imaginative staging helps tackle the empirical gap, whether we understand this gap as humans' distance from the problem more broadly on an everyday level or our distance from the problem quite specifically as spectators are contemplating the major issues within the often confining structure of a theatre space. As Lonergan observes, the positioning of a theatre

[3] As I discuss in detail elsewhere, the airport as representative of acts of revelation and transgression and always as an ethically and morally loaded locale recurs in Stephens's work, primarily in *Wastwater* and *T5* (2011) and *Song from Far Away* (2015), whose title is reminiscent of Churchill's play. See Angelaki, Vicky. *Social and Political Theatre in 21st-Century Britain: Staging Crisis*. Bloomsbury, 2017.

production is no less significant than the play's narrative itself and part of why humans have been so ineffective against rising temperatures is that refusing to acknowledge reality has always been a tempting possibility. And while it is inevitable to wonder to what extent larger-scale interventions along the lines of the Corcadorca example may be pragmatically possible – given the real limitations on material resources and the sustainability of such shows – so that they might reach a genuinely broad audience, it is equally important to keep in mind that paradigms do exist. Similarly, it is the business not only of festivals, as was the case for this production and the Cork Midsummer Festival, to take climate change shows out of the building but also of programming theatres themselves, given that the bulk of environmentally aware shows still take place within four walls. At times, this focus on the building as primary space might strike us as rather counterintuitive given the topic at hand.

In other cases, the dystopia was rendered visible and at times almost unbearable, because cultural differences are also reflected in the approaches that playwrights have taken towards representing the realities of climate change. A recent example of a text no less aggressive in its critique of complacency than Ibsen's timeless paradigm, though it followed a significantly more graphic visual path towards representing it, is Thomas Köck's *paradies fluten* [*flooding paradise*] (2016). The piece forms part of the *Klimatrilogie* [climate trilogy] *paradies fluten/paradies hungern/paradies spielen* [*flooding paradise/starving paradise/playing paradise*]. Although the piece received its premiere in Germany's

Ruhrfestspiele Recklinghausen, Köck himself is Austrian, which is significant for understanding the literary and artistic traditions that he forms part of.

Köck's text, which fluctuates in form throughout and occasionally includes brief references in languages other than German, is evocative of Elfriede Jelinek's *Textflächen*. Though not quite as untameable as Jelinek's textual surfaces [the closest translation for the German term], which correspond to expansive mental spaces of meaning and conceptualisation, Köck's play deviates considerably from the norm of dramatic text and moves into substantial experimentation territory, such that we are largely kept at a distance from traditional modes of dialogue. All the while, the historical reference and universal referentiality of the play are maintained, helping it make a strong sociopolitical statement. The production that I saw in September 2017 was staged at Vienna's Akademietheater, part of the heavily subsidised Burgtheater, which, significantly, still invests in radical experimentation (as with the previously discussed Ibsen example). The director, Robert Borgmann, and the dramaturg, Eva-Maria Voigtländer, went some way towards meeting the challenge of the text. Textual surfaces and flows were matched by a large-scale visual canvas that struck a chord with other aspects of Austrian representational art, which also function on the basis of unruly releases. In the specific production, these releases were both verbal and visual. The result was a theatrical tableau vivant of episodes in human excess and catastrophe, devastation and isolation, as a radical form of representing the Anthropocene.

paradies fluten at the Akademietheater was visually precise, exploring the consequences of human interference with resources and offering a dissection of humanity's path towards eventual extinction. In that sense, it was on its own adventurous trail towards a new form of radical naturalism for the twenty-first century. But there were other discernible influences too, this time more abstract. The visceral character of the piece and the forceful intermingling of different narrative forms emulated the means and mood of Viennese Actionism [*Wiener Aktionismus*], where the body was deployed as the means and method for capturing, through abstract expressionism, social uncertainties and crises. The canvas in Köck's piece is human greed. As the performance opens, we encounter a post-apocalyptic landscape where all resources have been drained, and we are faced with two hollow shells of humanity, outlandish, surveying the field beyond any scope of redemption. The women we encounter could be the evolution of Beckettian figures, their long hair, ghostly appearance, silence and later stark repetition an obvious nod to the dramatist. The play then stages the histories of colonialism (particular reference is made to Brazil and the draining of resources); of genocide and violence against Indigenous populations; of middle-class complacency, across time; and of multiple transgressions against nature and fellow human beings. All the while, play and production combine the sleek with the grotesque and the verbal with the sensory in explosive combinations. During one particularly memorable scene on the evening I attended, several members of an audience that had already, in parts, audibly expressed that they felt awkward, began to walk out mid performance. In the interval immediately following the specific episode and prior to the return for the final, anti-climactic sequence and as the theatre crew were meticulously cleaning the stage, a member of the audience remained in the auditorium and entered a protracted performance of slow, loud applause that, as gradually became obvious, was a form of protest, presumably against the piece. Such reactions are particularly uncommon in Vienna, where audiences typically not only stay for the entirety of a given show but also applaud extensively in the finale as part of a social convention. What had caused so strong a reaction was the preceding lengthy scene, featuring a number of actors separated, also highly uncommonly, from the audience by means of a transparent net. The net was placed to protect spectators from the projection of fluids – red, to indicate blood – that intensified as the scene itself unfolded increasingly violently, staging consumption and destruction as part of a vicious circle, in what we might imagine as one last excessive capitalist orgy. A post-apocalyptic Last Supper of sorts. Dealing with the question of how to represent an unfolding crisis whose repercussions have not yet been fully felt, let alone dealt with, this production attacked the dilemma by evidencing how profoundly destructive and disturbing the violation of nature might look. The stage image was both a metaphor, to be imagined on a larger scale, and a literal representation in itself. It was as captivating as it was frightening, as affective as it was appalling.

In recent years, beyond singular efforts, there has also been significant movement in collective playwriting initiatives.

A leader on this front has been Climate Change Theatre Action, which has enabled cohesive artistic collaboration on the topic of theatre and climate change through genuinely internationalist exchange. Climate Change Theatre Action recognises that different stakeholders will have different means but disallows factors such as resources, access and privilege to act as hindrances of participation. The premise is relatively straightforward: Climate Change Theatre Action invites interested parties to host an event that might be a reading, full performance or anything in between, in front of an audience, of a play that takes on climate change as a core concern. In terms of identifying a suitable play, Climate Change Theatre Action facilitates the participants' process by making a recommendation and providing texts for 50 plays of short length, though each participant is responsible for securing their own funding.

Every two years, Climate Change Theatre Action delivers its activity as a multinational (in that sense mirroring UN events) satellite action to the political gatherings that are designed to move forward global action on climate change. In 2017, for example, events took place from October to November, in the context of COP Bonn, which ran from 6 to 17 November. Significantly, the internationalism of the collective is reflected not only in the worldwide participation that it promotes but also in the curation of the base of plays that the participants are invited to select from. In this way, Climate Change Theatre Action emerges as one of the most democratic initiatives developed around theatre and environment, representative of the issue as it is experienced not only in the resource-heavy West but also in considerably more challenged and, in many cases, impoverished parts of the world. As Chantal Bilodeau – playwright, originator of the blog *Arts and Climate Change* and one of the core organisers of Climate Change Theatre Action – notes, attracting attention from different directions was crucial to the conception of the collective event, which began with the highly publicised COP21 (Paris). In 2017, the 50 plays featured spoke to the internationalism of the initiative, with countries represented including Australia, Brazil, Canada, Ethiopia, Fiji, India, Kenya, Lebanon, New Zealand, Pakistan, Uganda, the United Kingdom and the United States. In addition, a number of pieces with dual or multiple provenance included: Canada/the United States; Canada/Dene/Inuvialuit; Canada/New Zealand/Maori; Canada/Japan; Canada/Nlaka'pamux; New Zealand/Maori; New Zealand/Samoa; the United Kingdom/Iraq; Germany/Jordan; Australia/Zimbabwe; the United States/Philippines/Spain; the United States/Greece; the United States/Romania (Climate Change Theatre Action). For the same round of the event, the producing countries were as follows: Argentina, Australia, Austria, Barbados, Botswana, Brazil, Canada, Chile, China, Columbia, Czech Republic, Denmark, Egypt, France, Greece, India, Ireland, Japan, Kenya, Lebanon, Lithuania, Mexico, Nepal, New Zealand, Nigeria, Pakistan, Peru, Poland, Romania, Saint Lucia, Senegal, Singapore, South Africa, Togo, the United Arab Emirates, the United Kingdom and the United States (Climate Change Theatre Action).

The core team behind Climate Change Theatre Action in its 2015 beginnings consisted of Elaine Ávila, Caridad Svich and Bilodeau. All co-founders have significant histories of artistic activism as writers and members of collectives who have taken on topical sociopolitical concerns as pivots for their work, concentrating a lot of the time on environmental issues. Those other collectives are Theatre without Borders (Ávila), No Passport (theatre alliance and press – Svich, founder) and The Arctic Cycle (Bilodeau, founder). Bilodeau credits Roberta Levitow (Theatre without Borders) for her catalytic impact on the project's growth, as she provided a path to writers based in different corners of the world ('As the Climate Change Threat Grows'). Such was the mission statement of Theatre without Borders: creating possibilities for cultural bridges and collaboration across countries and continents. One can hardly call nascent an ambitious event that has already run twice, but for the purposes of staging histories and long-term narratives, Climate Change Theatre Action, taking place in 2015 and 2017, with the next instalment planned for 2019, is still a relatively new initiative. It is, to say the least, encouraging to witness such an activity take hold in a way that indeed transcends borders and works towards addressing and counterbalancing – at least in the artistic domain – the injustices in the distribution of agency and power when it comes to global players on the political stage of climate change.

Climate Change Theatre Action relies on its contributors to provide their labour and support to the cause, indeed, on their own resources, and, in that sense, it is not an altogether infallible model. But if we recognise that, however imperfect the project, it still represents activity against passivity and embodies art and artists' ability to mobilise communities towards participating in a dialogue, taking a pluralist rather than exclusive approach in such a way that it brings to the issue the public-facing, global treatment that it merits in high volumes, then Climate Change Theatre Action must be judged overwhelmingly positively. The event is a form of outsourcing; but a lack of substantial and sustained funding proves a hindrance too often, leading, also too often, to absence and silence. Climate Change Theatre Action appears to have found a way towards restoring a presence and a voice, sidestepping the usual blockages. Its greatest value and its future potential are perhaps to be found in the words of Bilodeau, who describes Climate Change Theatre Action as 'a global movement' ('As the Climate Change Threat Grows'). If climate change were indeed to be adopted more widely as a cause, in a way that is truly intercultural and non-partisan, a standing discourse rather than ephemeral conversation, then the futures and legacies of the project have the potential to be game-changers.

Directors and Companies

This section necessarily maintains a link to the one preceding it but also to the ensuing one, which opens up to performative installation more specifically. It is fitting to begin this part of the book, which concentrates on directors and companies who have adopted a distinctly environmental agenda, with Katie Mitchell's significant contribution.

By the time *2071* was staged at the Royal Court, a co-production with the Deutsches Schauspielhaus Hamburg, which also produced Rimini Protokoll's then new piece, *Welt-Klimakonferenz/World Climate Change Conference* in the same 2014–2015 season, the environmental crisis seemed almost irretrievably dire. Running at slightly under 90 minutes, *2071*, co-created by Mitchell, environmental scientist Chris Rapley and playwright Duncan Macmillan, revealed the consequences of human excess at the expense of the planet. Like *Ten Billion* (2012), the product of collaboration between Mitchell and scientist Stephen Emmott, before it, *2071* took the form of a performance lecture. Both pieces focused on delivering a straightforward message on our complicity in the global climate crisis in which we have entangled not only ourselves but also future generations.

The transition from the more intimate Royal Court Theatre Upstairs (*Ten Billion*) to the Theatre Downstairs (*2071*) was itself an indication of how public awareness of the environment issue had changed in the meantime. It also revealed a certain confidence on the part of the Royal Court that a performance lecture could generate a substantial enough audience to fill its main space. Where *Ten Billion* had been an experiment, *2071* was a certainty. While the former had received some attention in the press, the latter was treated as a major event, with increased publicity. After *2071* had completed its initial run in Britain in November 2014, the Royal Court brought it back in January 2015 'due to overwhelming demand … for three shows only' ('2071'). The language was no different from that used to promote any other show, even though this particular one was very different from the usual West End spectacular in scope, form and subject matter. Clearly, the environment and an impending crisis larger than anything we have previously experienced could sell tickets. Even more than that, the show's success demonstrated that there was a growing need to come together as a community and reflect.

Ten Billion, which, further to its London staging, also received a transfer to France's Avignon festival, had prepared the way, a significant step in a broader spectrum of artistic choices that indicated Mitchell was becoming a theatre and environment activist with influence over international programming agendas. One year earlier, also at the Royal Court (Theatre Downstairs), Mitchell had directed the premiere of Simon Stephens's *Wastwater* (2011). Our world of increased mobility and diminishing distances, as well as the growing internationalisation of modern working and private lives, which characterised Mitchell's own experience, appeared to have a decisive impact on her choices, spurring her eco-conscience. In the autumn of 2014, shortly before the premiere of *2071* and as Deutsche Bahn, the German national rail carrier, announced that it would terminate night trains connecting major European cities, reducing the service of its remaining lines and following on from yet more reductions of such services by European rail operators (Oltermann), Mitchell wrote a heartfelt text for the *Guardian*. She reflected on her life as a mobile artist to build a case as to why night trains were crucial for the preservation of some balance in a world now overwhelmingly reliant on air travel. Mitchell has also noted that she 'stopped flying in 2011' in addition to other actions such as dedicated recycling and not buying new clothes, and credited *Ten Billion* as a catalyst for this change (Merritt). Mitchell's statement made a case for the ideologically and behaviourally transformative potential of theatre. Rather than relegating responsibility for change, Mitchell actively took on the task of preserving resources through her own contribution. The director identified the urgency of environmental preservation for future generations as a key factor for her lifestyle shift, citing her travelling on night trains with her young daughter as a poignant reminder of why such forms of travel needed to survive (Mitchell). As Mitchell also characteristically remarks, it is our responsibility to acknowledge that we are 'accountable' for the future state of the world, rather than mere passive observers (Merritt).

This concern is, of course, of particular relevance to the theatre, and *2071* was highly reflective of the fact. A piece that could on occasion feel rigid in delivery as well as facts, the rare emotionalism that it allowed arose from Rapley's references to his childhood while contemplating the state of the world when his eldest granddaughter, Josephine, to whom the script is dedicated, will be at the same age as he is at the time of performance: 67. That date is 2071. As with Mitchell's night train experience, the public problem is shown to be a private one and vice versa. At the heart of the environmental crisis lies the human: instigator, recipient and manager. The term 'manager' is more apt because, as Rapley notes, this is not about a reversal of what has already been destroyed. It is about stopping short of a catastrophe that is objectively calculable on the precedent of humanity's existing habits (Royal Court Play). Prior to *2071* Macmillan had explored this concern in *Lungs* (2011), albeit from a different lens. In that case, the plot is focused on a couple and their quandary over diminishing natural resources, as they are deliberating over whether to have a child. Tellingly, Mitchell directed a production of the play, translated as *Atmen* (meaning 'to breathe', or 'breathing') and premiering in 2013, at the Schaubühne Berlin. For this staging, two actors placed on podiums/capacitors pedalled on their static bicycles to power the entire show with the help of four more production staff members pedalling on A-frame bicycles at the edge of either side of the stage. This production fleshed out the environmental resonance of the play with greater urgency than the traditional dialogical model that most productions of *Lungs* have followed before or after. The question is suitably complex. With parenthood, *Lungs* suggests, responsibility shifts. The conversation still concerns prevention, but now, arguably, with an even more pronounced investment in the future of others. On the other hand, overpopulation becomes a greater risk for the planet as a whole when couples, such as the one shown in Macmillan's play, decide to have children. Similarly, although *2071* was graphically presenting the excesses that have already made a mark on the planet, it was largely geared towards the future. This future was envisaged both as long term, through a reflection on what could still be changed while humanity transitions to the next stage in is history, and as short term, through the anchoring of the show's narrative on the UN Climate Change Conference in Paris in December 2015. As Rapley points out, an effective and bold intervention at this crucial junction would 'require the greatest collective action in history' (Billington).

Communicating this to an audience was a challenge in itself, and *2071* only narrowly escaped what might be described as the gloominess of *Ten Billion*. Such was the pitfall that the creative team sought to avoid – that is, a show too dark to instigate hope (Merritt). Mitchell, Macmillan and Rapley were aware of the need to make *2071* engaging, and finding a narrative structure was the first difficulty, because it meant reconciling contradictory working methods. As Rapley argues, where the writer seeks a narrative arc, the scientist does not (Macmillan, Mitchell, Rapley and Campbell). The shared objective of 'communicat[ing] to a new audience the science from ... [Rapley's] field without compromising any of it', as Macmillan reveals, took the better part of a year (Macmillan, Mitchell, Rapley and Campbell). *2071* remained unpublished during its first run, eventually becoming available as free download through the Royal Court website. In the meantime, an extensive piece by Rapley and Macmillan had been published in the *Guardian* delving into some of the facts explored in the show and following in its style: rich in somewhat simplified scientific data for the average non-expert to follow (Rapley and Macmillan). Perhaps surprisingly, given its form and approach, Rapley and Macmillan call *2071* not a dramatised lecture but a play, defining their objective as 'leav[ing] the audience better placed to participate in the public discourse' (Rapley and Macmillan).

Macmillan, Mitchell and Rapley's promotional discourse around *2071* allows the impression that this might have been imagined by its artistic team to be a more dialectically open show than it emerged as in its final version. By lack of openness, I mean both the structure of the event and, to an extent, the degree of optimism it encouraged. Mitchell described *2071* as the equivalent of 'having a chat with Chris in his living room' (Merritt). In my experience, the atmosphere in performance was somewhat different. The encounter was certainly direct, but it was also static and could occasionally feel one-sided. The fact that Rapley remained seated in the same armchair for the duration amplified this, and it was only the backdrop of the video projection running through the entire piece that offered any motion or sense of interactivity (Chloe Lamford was the set designer, with Luke Halls responsible for the video). Where *2071* differed from *Ten Billion* was in how it framed the future and how it imagined the spectator: with our everyday choices and inactions under the spotlight in both shows, at least *2071* allowed its spectators the option of conceptualising themselves as reformed perpetrators. We were in for a difficult ride, but the show placed some faith in the community of citizens gathering to listen and potentially intervene through actions and adjustments in our everyday lives. Blind optimism, after all, would have been irresponsible and ethically problematic given the social remit of the show.

Clearly, the major concern of *2071* was to create the impression of a story, a vested interest, as well as a climax that would be the call to collective action coinciding with our realisation of its urgent necessity. *Ten Billion* was the first step in this new direction of Mitchell's theatre, and Mitchell and Emmott had considered numerous options before settling on a stage that reproduced Emmott's office – 'a dump full of papers and piles of old journals' ('Overpopulation') – with a format that involved Emmott delivering facts and even improvising (Perrier). Emmott tentatively described *Ten Billion* as 'not really a play', given that he would not learn lines like an actor, but rather, he would present data, with Mitchell responsible for setting the rhythm of the show ('Overpopulation'). Although different from *2071* in that it did not enlist a playwright to bring structure to facts and formulate a narrative, *Ten Billion* shared the style of *2071* in that there was no mediation between scientist and spectator, only direct confrontation. Mitchell describes the show as an entirely new form, an experience between theatrical event and academic conference (Perrier). By staging the scientist and foregoing the actor, *Ten Billion* and *2071* maximised what is specific to the theatre as form and forum: it conditions us to listen differently than we would in a public lecture or an academic conference. Emmott and Rapley's respective data, then, presented in a theatre auditorium for the audience to ponder on, immediately acquired an amplified reach, emphasising adjustments to the way we live our lives that, if undertaken widely, hold the potential for considerable effect.

Ten Billion prioritised overpopulation and *2071* energy, but their overall canvas was one and the same: the natural world and the pressing need for a redefinition of our relationship to it. *2071* had an edge partly because of social factors – developments in public discourse that created a buildup to the inevitable realisation that we are players in a critical historical moment – and partly because of dramaturgical ones. Specifically, *2071* found a better way of making the environment our story, not by pointing the finger but by inviting us into a dialogue, albeit one that the nature of the piece did not enable to take place during performance. Ultimately, though, both texts were interventionist, instructive pieces of theatre. They pushed formal boundaries to accommodate scientific discourse not seeking to create the abstraction typically associated with text-based theatrical innovation but quite the opposite: theatre with a message, but for a new era of spectators who had grown weary of familiar methods and traditional speeches. Where *Ten Billion* was an attack of facts, *2071* lured us in through the sharing of experiences, which, all things considered, made the sheer volume of data easier to engage with.

Similarly ambitious in coverage, if substantially more open to, and indeed reliant on, audience interaction, was Rimini Protokoll's *Welt-Klimakonferenz* (*World Climate Change Conference*), opening at the Deutsches Schauspielhaus Hamburg in November 2014. The project was a direct theatrical precursor to COP 21, and consequently, it emulated the global, collective and democratic sociopolitical event it anticipated. As spectators were informed on the evening of

12 December 2014, the performance also coincided with the final day of COP 20 in Lima (*Welt-Klimakonferenz*, the same source also informing ensuing references to the specifics of the show). This reinforced the urgency of arriving at a collaborative decision on a dual level: the theatre and political action. The two became closely intertwined for spectators attending Rimini Protokoll's show, for which they were asked to imagine themselves as representatives of country delegations – one person in each smaller group being assigned the role of delegation head. The audience/delegates benefited from the guidance of experts, who would enter into a dialogue with them, informing them about the particular context and challenges for a given country concerned/represented.

The structure of the event was relatively complex. Other than delegation instructions, spectators were also given booklets indicating their list and timetable of actions for the evening. Three of these would be dealt with in breakout sessions (each focused on a different subtopic), which would take place in various spaces within the theatre before reconvening in the main auditorium. Through such performance/co-working devices, the show evoked the methods of the actual conference. Audience members were advised that there was no room for deviation from the programme and that it was crucial that they kept to allocated times. The goal for all delegations/spectators was the same: to arrive at an agreement, first regional and then global, serving the target of managing the world's rising temperature and 2°C maximum increase challenge. Consequently, the coordinative logistics of the show were as remarkable as its scope.

Welt-Klimakonferenz did not take a symbolic approach to the universality of the issue but rather a corporeal and literal one, with bodies at work on the ground: from discussions about to simulations of climate change conditions, this was a densely lived rather than merely live event. All the while the show enlisted, as Mitchell's work had also been doing, the contribution of scientists, from whom regional delegations would hear directly. The performativity of the interaction with these experts was boosted through the tone of immediacy that the speakers took, the direct audience engagement and occasional interactivity, especially in the smaller spaces, and the physicality of their delivery. The promenade/rotational and spatially experiential format of *Welt-Klimakonferenz* made it innovative and significant, causing it to stand out within the realm of environmentally geared performance because of its conceptualisation, ambition and execution equally. The mobility embedded in the event further accentuated primary concerns: from reducing geographical distances within the remit of the piece, therefore highlighting the problem as not remote but of our own here and now, to suggesting that our proprietary and appropriating attitudes towards the planet, manifested in our increased mobility, ought to be re-examined. What does it mean, after all, not only to inhabit, or pass through a city or country, and indeed a theatre as international as the Schauspielhaus Hamburg, but also to bear prime responsibility and agency?

Welt-Klimakonferenz took the term 'multimedia' to a new level, better understood as 'multimodal'. Technologies were applied (screens with data as well as footage; various staging effects; reports live from Lima; mobility facilitators, such as the bus that served as one of the breakout spaces), but they were only part of a complex and nuanced mode of seeing and participating, in which the spectator/citizen remained the primary agent. An additional factor that causes *Welt-Klimakonferenz* to stand out is its combination of exposure to facts and of collective conversation, not least focused on sustained solutions, commitment and action. Whereas the most successful environmental performances will always encourage reflection, it is not necessarily the case that the theatre will also offer a space and opportunity for this to happen vocally as part of the piece itself, encouraging equal contribution from fellow spectators, especially in a way that emerges naturally rather than feeling extraneous. Overall, through the experts' and the audience's respective roles, the piece struck a notably activist tone. The negotiations, deliberations and commitments that led to the delegations' declarations of intent, submitted by each group and summed up in the closing plenary, reinforced democracy as a tool not only for action but also for spectatorship. In practice, this made the most of the theatre as a gathering space (reflected in the shape of the Schauspielhaus auditorium) while imagining the totality of the theatre building – including its temporary, mobile, affiliated spaces – as the quintessential forum of a local and international community sharing the same goal.

The work of Katie Mitchell and Rimini Protokoll gives rise to a set of questions concerning the options and responsibilities that theatres face towards promoting environmental awareness, as well as the concrete actions they take towards implementing this turn. As we will see in the next section, one aspect of this process is infrastructure, meaning green, or at least greener, buildings. The venues that have commissioned and hosted work by Mitchell and Rimini Protokoll that has concentrated on overpopulation and climate change are all established, institutional spaces, housed in permanent structures of relatively reduced flexibility. If a company or a director is going to act as an architect of environmental theatre, then, among the primary parameters of this effort, spatial transformation is key. The theatre needs to be seen through fresh eyes. For Mitchell, this was better achieved at the Schaubühne than at the Royal Court, for example. However institutional, the Schaubühne offers more options for spatial reimaginings, enabling the relative erasure of a border between performers and audience. The lack of costume, as the performers in *Atmen* were dressed in exercise gear, further challenged traditional spectating conventions, forging the impression that the performers' labour was also ours and that we were partaking in the effort, which could, metaphorically, be interpreted as the race to save the planet. The concept of a shared space – and consequently the implications of a shared environment – was somewhat compromised in the Royal Court shows which maintained traditional spatial organisational principles of stage and auditorium.

However significant and indeed essential the social gesture of shows like *Ten Billion* and *2071* is, we ought to consider whether the form of the performance lecture is the most affective for the theatre of climate change or whether more avenues need to be explored towards methods of incorporating expert scientific opinion into performance. The Rimini Protokoll method went some way towards transforming the spectators' mode of engagement and interaction with the Schauspielhaus Hamburg and with one another. Beyond any aesthetic tropes of promenade performance or worn-out audience participation methods, spectators came together as problem solvers, with a task relating to a concern impacting well beyond the immediate locus of performance or the show at hand. The 'conference' became a community deciding on prerogatives that, if nothing else, informed audiences about the options available, as well as the stakes and hindrances. Overall, despite varying degrees of successful experimentation and shortcomings revealing lingering awkwardness as to how to incorporate scientific data into performance, the interventions of the Royal Court, the Schaubühne Berlin and the Schauspielhaus Hamburg continue to be exemplary in setting the tone for how major subsidised theatre companies might commission work that is popular with audiences while fostering awareness on climate change in an activist manner.

As with scholarship, so with performance, it is important to consider roots and antecedents. In a relatively early contribution to the field of performance and ecology, Stephen Bottoms and Matthew Goulish concentrated on the work of the Chicago-based company Goat Island, which Goulish co-founded in 1987. Their book, *Small Acts of Repair: Performance, Ecology and Goat Island*, offers an understanding of the ecologies and environments of performance mindful of localities, synergies and ecosystems beyond the strictly defined terms of theatre conceived around overpopulation, resource saturation and climate change. Bottoms and Goulish intertwine environmentally geared performance and the experience of social and spatial ecologies as encountered in our daily lives as citizens – in our familiar locales and cities, for example. It is particularly telling that their prescience in how capitalist hierarchies and oligarchies impact spatial and social ecologies, affecting the everyday performances of cities and people, as well as their changing landscapes (natural or otherwise), leads them to quote Félix Guattari (Bottoms and Goulish 32) in a reference he makes to Donald Trump (2000). This, of course, comes well before Trump became president of the United States and declared his country's break with the 2015 Paris Agreement. Quoting the Guattari reference, made as the planet was transitioning to a new century of extraordinary challenges, in a book published in 2007, so that the Trump influence is metaphorically framed on natural environment terms, accounting for what Guattari presents as the adverse effect of his business on vulnerable social strata, is today beyond poignant. I leave Guattari's text here to speak for itself:

> *In the field of social ecology, men like Donald Trump are permitted to proliferate freely, like another species of algae, taking over entire districts of New York*

and Atlantic City; he 'redevelops' by raising rents, thereby driving out tens of thousands of poor families, most of whom are condemned to homelessness, becoming the equivalent of the dead fish of environmental ecology.

(Bottoms and Goulish 32; original emphasis)

It is significant to note the nuanced approach that the work of Goat Island took to concerns of the individual as part of their natural world, particularly in *It's Shifting, Hank* (1994); *The Sea and Poison* (1997); *It's an Earthquake in My Heart* (1999); and *When Will the September Roses Bloom? Last Night Was Only a Comedy* (2002) (dates given indicate the first performance, including as work in progress). Respectively, these works deal with the body striving to adapt while displaying physical and especially respiratory struggle; the side effects of exposure (particularly contamination) to harmful chemicals and substances at the individual level and on a large scale; physicality, resilience and adaptability in modes of relating to one's environment, broadly conceived; and the concept of interventionist action towards reversing destruction. Different forms of disruption to biorhythms, then, provided a consistent line informing the work of Goat Island. In the context of other practices considered in this book, it is particularly worth noting, beyond similarities of broader, recurring themes among environmentally aware theatre-makers, the distinct physicalities of the body under duress developing in the work of Goat Island and

Katie Mitchell alike. *It's Shifting, Hank*, with its emphasis on breathing and expiring as a laborious process of examination and precision, links to Mitchell's work in *Lungs*: particularly so as *Atmen* at the Schaubühne, where the performers' laboured breathing, testing of natural boundaries and intensification of activity both served and transcended character, commanding attention as a coordinated but also individual act of resilience and survival in itself, singularly, as well as socially conceptualised.

If Goat Island were concluding their activity as a collective towards the end of the previous decade, Phantom Limb Company were just beginning in New York, where Jessica Grindstaff and Erik Sanko came together to develop work with marionettes/puppetry and multimedia. Ecological concerns serve as common ground for the company and their diverse projects, and Phantom Limb have developed substantial outreach activity by staging their practice in different corners of the world. The company particularly foregrounds their 'trilogy' (Grindstaff and Sanko), consisting of *69°S* (2011), *Memory Rings* (2016) and *Falling Out* (2018, forthcoming as this book was being finalised), as particularly motivated by and responsive to the environmental crisis, although it is fair to say that their work is never far removed from this scope. Their dystopian piece *Flesh and Blood and Fish and Fowl* (2008), for example, exposed the anthropocentric dimension to ecological imbalance identified by Chaudhuri, as we have seen, as being at the heart of the problem. It explored the question of what happens when those entities that humans might deem utilitarian, subservient and of reduced agency are no longer under control. *Flesh and Blood and Fish and Fowl* delivered a theatrical protest against the suppression and conquest of wildlife and nature more broadly. It depicted the process of nature reclaiming its own, as the stage underwent transformation into an increasingly wilder state that was as unnerving as it was astute, teasing the boundaries of human nature built on capitalism. Ultimately, animal nature prevailed with irrepressible force.

Phantom Limb's trilogy makes an equally compelling case for how theatre companies working today may not only shine a light on the issue of climate change through their work but, importantly, also sustain this prerogative over a period of time. *69°S* (alternative title: *The Shackleton Project*), which the company describes as a 'painterly narrative installation-in-motion' (Grindstaff and Sanko), delivered a visually striking performance that was stylistically impressive and thematically on point. The central reference was Sir Ernest Shackleton's Trans-Atlantic 'Endurance' expedition (1914), which proved both extraordinarily arduous and a testament to will for survival and endurance under extreme conditions. The performance, for which the company collaborated with the Kronos Quartet, showcased Phantom Limb's somatic emphasis, with scenography and choreography as storytelling pivots. It created a visually and aurally tense stage environment and audience experience geared towards crisis and dissolution. The sound of Kronos Quartet's intrusive and unnerving melody, amplified by the live delivery of the band Skeleton Key, offered more than a musical accompaniment, taking an active role in storytelling. The grotesque aesthetics of large puppets and their exaggerated physicality, each movement precise and purposeful, combined with the blankness and artificiality of the masks representing human explorers, suited the case that the piece was making. This hinged on gradual distortion, fragmentation and dissipation, creating meaningful moments of interaction between the human and the non-human that were evocative of the turn away from anthropocentrism as a methodological tool and, at the same time, of the decreasing resilience of humanity as a direct consequence of its own depletion of resources.

Ultimately, that which we presume to be human (the members of the expedition) is revealed to be an elaborate marionette; that which we assume to be a marionette, the non-human figure in white reminiscent of the icicles on set, in fact holds the strings (in reality, an actor on stilts), controlling the actual marionette. Visual assumptions based on normative structures and performance reality therefore contradicted each other, radically undermining the human as protagonist. In this piece too, nature asserted itself. In Phantom Limb's view, 'the puppeteer ... [becomes] a benevolent entity faithfully guiding his ward through a fascinatingly harsh environment' (Grindstaff and Sanko). Their performance represented the ferocity of the natural element against human presence, employing one of theatre's most potent devices: the historical paradigm as contemporary metaphor. In this way, the show captured both the shifting unpredictability of an increasingly hostile landscape that is now unsuitable for human presence and the human instinct to explore and conquer nature, bowing to its ultimate dominance. Both the current crisis and the need to imagine ourselves as an agent for its management, albeit not as the protagonist in natural biorhythms, were thoughtfully represented. Ultimately, despite the dramatic uncertainty, the message of the piece remains hopeful; such is the story that it is framed upon, one of strenuous collaboration and perseverance. If Shackleton's crew are saved, then perhaps there is a moral to extract: once the goal is collectively assumed, however impossible it may seem, however the odds may be stacked against it, the project may endure and deliver. The project, in the current moment, is managing the planet's temperature against the most demanding of circumstances. In performance, we have seen Shackleton's team guided by the puppets representing the landscape (icicles). As this piece manifested, if nature acts as the guide today too, we might discover a way forward yet.

Five years after their radical stage rendition of the Shackleton expedition, Phantom Limb brought the second part of their environmental trilogy to their audience. *Memory Rings* trod in familiar Phantom Limb territory, using the company's trademark tools of choreography, thoughtful soundscapes, puppets, masks and natural landscapes erupting on the stage to tell of forest discoveries. Unruly objects and non-human life forms once more undermined anthropocentrism. From ice as responsive but also unpredictable variable displaying anthropomorphic features of resilience and, equally, fragility, as it can be both permanent and transient, focus shifted to the tree. The tree serves as another powerful signifier and enduring register of natural and human experience, reflecting, through the state of its survival, the prevailing environmental conditions. Moreover, the tree equally forms part of a human-inhabited landscape and is a force unto itself. If, in *69°S*, humans intermeshed with nature appearing in costume emulating icicles and in stilts implying at the same time non-human artificiality, here human features gave way to animal ones. For parts of the show, company members appeared in full mask, representing animal heads. As with Shackleton, here too we were dealing with an epic paradigm of survival, though in this case, it is the tree that serves as its symbol.

The company cite their inspiration as 'Dendrochronology' (Grindstaff and Sanko), a term that from *dendron* [tree], *chronos* [time] and *logos* [discourse, also reason] delivers a field and method for documenting experience synchronically and diachronically. The act of subverting anthropocentrism in this case relies on identifying a non-human living entity, whose agency and authority are foregrounded rather than deemed secondary, as a unit of logging and quantifying time and history. Viewed semiotically, the tree is one of the most powerful symbols of nature. It is also, however, a primary resource for exploitation and can be understood as raw material destined for everyday utilitarian use. Phantom Limb's dystopian fairy tale identifies the world's oldest surviving tree as its grounding point, intertwined with the story of Gilgamesh, in itself surviving through centuries as a narrative of human will. According to critics and the company's framing of the piece, this narrative of bravery, however, also involved practices of extensive deforestation (Grindstaff and Sanko).

Meanwhile, the interjection of recognisable fairy tales, most notably *Little Red Riding Hood*, asks us to reconceptualise what it is about the human conquering the natural that is so alluring in literary and historical mythologies – so much so, in fact, that it has become the dominant narrative. As the piece allows us to imagine, such deeply rooted genealogies of storytelling forge stereotypes of non-human wilderness and ferocity set against the noble perseverance of the human who is not necessarily by default bold or brave but who manages nonetheless to rise to the occasion and emerge as a hero. We must also bear in mind, *Memory Rings* makes clear, that this individual may equally plausibly be interpreted as an intruder. Therefore, as a receiving audience, it is our responsibility to question the validity of humans' so-called instincts to tame nature, which is often one-sidedly conceptualised in anthropomorphic mode as hostile and aggressive. It takes the rings of time on the tree, silent yet potent testimonies of resilience, to reverse the dominant histories propagated by the self-proclaimed victor, the human.

As this book was being written, Phantom Limb were developing the final part of their trilogy, *Falling Out*, inspired by Butoh practices and investigating the impact of bombings and radiation, drawing on the cultural and political history of Japan, set to premiere in 2018 (Grindstaff and Sanko). In their introduction to the work in progress and summation of the trilogy to date, Phantom Limb adopt a markedly activist tone, describing their practice as community aware and incentive for their spectators to consider their own lifestyle choices, identifying options for making a difference within given local contexts (Grindstaff and Sanko). Phantom Limb's ability to rediscover stories, histories and objects and integrate them not merely into multimedia but multi-method new pieces to draw spectators to theatre that deals with climate change is admirable. Irrespective of how a company might frame its work, however, ultimately the actions that it may elicit on a civic level are particularly challenging to track; therefore any statements as to the community impact of the work must be treated as tentative. The trilogy (in its two-part incarnation as considered here) has garnered praise (McNulty) but also criticism (Grode, Isherwood) that, however abrasive it might appear, does legitimately raise the question whether, at the end, the multimodality serves beyond the point of artistic exercise to deliver work as astute and responsive as the company proclaims it to be. Wherever we may stand in relation to Phantom Limb's work, though, the visual and aural pluralism of their practice is distinctive, as is their ideological internationalism, which is particularly significant given the topic at hand. How these pieces that are both rooted in history and purposefully reflective of the present might transition into the future, however, remains to be established.

Public Art, Communities and Citizen Initiatives

The environment and nature have always incited public intervention. A lot of the time this has been accompanied by an element of the spectacular responding to everyday and institutionalised performances of consumption excess as their counteraction. We have encountered different examples – among them are potent advertising campaigns, shocking images that expose humans' cruelty towards the earth and the ecosystem and eco-activists deploying their bodies as vehicles of resistance against industrial transgressions. In the recent period, artistic and citizen initiatives have acquired a new sense of scale, increasing in number, impact and coverage. At the same time, considerately installed large-scale artworks have created a feeling of standing performance on theatre and climate change, engaging the spectator in an act of durational watching. The encounter of the artwork in the public space is significant not only because it reaches a broader audience but also because this audience is likely to be more diverse and often less informed than the kind of spectator who is well versed in climate change discourse and will make purposeful choices of self-exposure to relevant theatre repertoire or artistic endeavours.

Jason deCaires Taylor's work has been installed internationally, from Mexico to Spain and from the Bahamas to the United Kingdom, responsive to water as a connector of national and international communities and as an entire world unto itself. The work depicts frames of everyday human activity – often complacent – rendered still and haunting in its underwater environment; moments of human crisis; and multitudes of bodies pointing to images of community or to proliferation that implies overpopulation. The implication is that every act we commit, whether we acknowledge this or not, is monumental because it contributes to a lifestyle that has direct bearing on the environment. Interacting organically with its immediate natural context, deCaires Taylor's sculpture embeds itself in the locus of installation, often forming part of an emerging biotope. It is responsive art, which not only engages the observer/spectator in participating in its performance but also offers itself up for the taking to the biorhythms of the ecosystem it shares in. Environmental preservation emerges as a driving force for the artist, who proposes that sculpture can be a form of preservation in itself ('Threats'). The distinctive underwater art (or art submerged in water, whose visibility might on occasion be tide-contingent) that is deCaires Taylor's brand may not be performance in the strictest of senses, but its representational element is incontestable, and its silent expression of an urgent invitation for action and education gestures towards interactivity and continuity in a narrative that involves the spectator. The movement of the tide offers up a new form of dialectics: from appearance to disappearance, the terms of the conversation forever variable, the discourse always open to participation.

DeCaires Taylor's hydro-cultural practice claims to have attracted multitudes of spectators throughout the world, bringing attention to the issues it highlights at local governmental levels while generating (tourist) revenue that might be reinvested in environmental initiatives ('Threats'). His installations aim, therefore, at creating innovation in organising and spectating, which, beyond witnessing, will also catalyse action. All the while, deCaires Taylor's work furnishes ecosystems with agents to which they may be receptive, sustaining their growth. Those agents – the sculptures – 'are individually designed using safe pH neutral materials with textured surfaces to create homes, breeding areas and protective spaces' ('Threats') and are therefore supportive of the growth of underwater flora and fauna. The sculptures themselves do not run the risk of becoming dislocated, as they are firmly embedded in their space of installation ('Threats'). As to how the afterlife and contribution of the project is framed, the artist additionally notes that the work has in some cases also been conducive to regeneration ('Threats'). It is revealing that the term that deCaires Taylor uses for work that, submerged into oceanic depths, has provided welcome ground for native fauna and flora to develop is 'colonised'. This is important because it is the foreign body that is claimed by nature, rather than the other way around, which has been the norm. DeCaires Taylor's work provides nature the opportunity to reclaim the agency that has been systematically removed from it, displaced by human interests. Moreover, the foreign body itself is amenable rather than dominant and rigid, the ultimate juxtaposition with financial interests that have imposed their de facto working practices on the exhausted natural domain.

As climate-related artistic intervention that relies on long-term availability and sustained presence is becoming increasingly popular, so too have events springing out of particular political moments pivotal to action on climate change proliferated, not merely marking an occasion but propagating the need for action. The promotion of this work has gained from emerging digital publishing platforms, including the wide reach of social media as mobilisation mechanism. The universality of these modes of interaction and dissemination and their urgency and topicality have been useful partners for the environmental cause in the arts. This is especially true given their predominantly free accessibility in many parts of the world, which provides a counterbalance for heavily financed industries working on the opposite end of the spectrum. Such technologies serve the need for coping with and sharing new data emerging constantly; they are cross-generational; they create new avenues for participation, whether digital, physical or, in some cases, both. Significant to such efforts, the blog *Artists and Climate Change* offers a log of a wide range of activities broadly emerging from the need to combat climate change.

As already mentioned, a landmark occasion around which a plethora of artistic and community events developed in the recent period have been the UN Climate Change Conferences and especially, given its legislative significance, the 2015 Paris conference. ARTCOP21, a major platform extending beyond the conference itself, running from September to December 2015 and offering a total of 551 events featuring 54 countries (*ARTCOP21*), is a primary example. The multicultural element of the initiative was one of its strongest advantages, for two primary reasons: first, it treated climate change not as a challenge yet to affect the Western world in ways visible and dramatic but as a real and present crisis; second, it steered clear of favouring the agency of privileged, developed parts of the world that might claim ownership over the experience of peoples and countries in developing parts of the world, whose living conditions have been the most dramatically affected by transgressive commerce and consumption practices. ARTCOP21, therefore, provided a balanced collaborative approach to the key issues, managing to engage a diverse audience well beyond institutional spaces.

Specifically, it promoted a 'cultural movement towards a carbon-neutral, clean future' (*ARTCOP21*). Built on the principle that 'Climate is culture' and on global participation, ARTCOP21 stated its mission as casting the issue of climate change as a shared cause for communities beyond the traditional political negotiating forums, lobbies and institutional think tanks (*ARTCOP21*). Its prerogatives, then, speak directly to the philosophy represented by Chaudhuri, which positions the climate as an essential and permanent lens. Like ARTCOP21, Australia-based CLIMARTE operates across a diverse range of artistic forms and contributors. Its staple event is the ART+CLIMATE=CHANGE festival. Having begun in 2015, it continued in 2017 with a month of events dedicated to fostering awareness and encouraging participation. It is not fair to propose that up until 2015 we were not seeing the environmental cause feature widely in an increasing number of artistic endeavours, which had the potential to instigate thought and change. Certainly, however, festivals of this magnitude in the radius of a global political event have had the potential for significant impact. Crucial to this was the behavioural shift that ARTCOP21, for example, geared its activities towards, one that, like other work concentrating on social action on climate change, located the issue in our ingrained attitudes towards the economy (*ARTCOP21*). Environmental crisis was to be seen not as part of a vacuum, as a broken narrative leading to a conundrum but rather as a pragmatic problem with a cause and an effect – and, consequently, with methods of managing it that included changes to everyday patterns of consumption and larger-scale governmental initiatives. A staple event for ARTCOP21, the ten-day residency at Gaîté lyrique, provided the international community with a space for reflection and participation through conversations, workshops and performances in a diverse programme.

A few days prior to the residency, 1–11 December 2015 (*ARTCOP21*), the power of the environment to mobilise citizens had once more become manifest in the Global Climate March (28 and 29 November 2015). This initiative staged a coordinated public welcome to world leaders in Paris that extended beyond the actual geographical physical space of the city itself ('Global Climate March'). While imagining Paris as a notional centre, the event unfolded in numerous urban spaces worldwide, claiming to have attracted participants in the region of 785,000 in more than 2300 marches taking place in over 175 countries ('Global Climate March'). The initiative also contributed a new chapter to the history of the non-utilitarian performativity of the quotidian object when a march was halted in Paris itself as the city was still reeling from the terrorist incidents of the previous month (in November 2015, coordinated attacks across Paris led to numerous casualties and delivered a global shock). In lieu of protesters, on 29 November 2015, over 10,000 pairs of shoes (Peltier cites the figure as 11,000) inhabited the Place de la République. As widely reported, further to the thousands of pairs of shoes positioned in one of Paris's most emblematic spaces by civilians, two pairs of shoes belonging to two prominent figures were also present: one 'for former UN Secretary General Ban Ki-moon and one for Pope Francis. Through this intervention on the public space, the oft-mentioned footprint symbolising human transgression on nature went from abstract and metaphorical to literal and physical.

The significance of the act was twofold. On the one hand, a substantial enough indication of how the footprint translates on real terms was staged through the shoes left for the world to see, photograph and share. Our agency was given materiality. On the other hand, the object, standing in for the individual, rendered them present in their absence, an act of silent and potent protest commenting on the everyday, almost like a painting by Magritte: the inanimate implies the animate but at the same time has an agency of its own. Ultimately, the protest was an act of solidarity and defiance. The collective installation also allowed the world to reflect on its own consumption, manifesting the full scale of disposable objects – a further nuance to the call towards resource efficiency. Perhaps the economy and the environment are not polar opposites after all, as long as we gear ourselves towards economising rather than overspending. The spare pairs of shoes were, in themselves, a signifier of excess and a public act of baring its extent, perhaps even an attempt at penance. Such demonstrations of active citizenship in the face of radical change suggest that there is rising global recognition for the need not only to adopt a cause but also to actively embody and represent it through organised participation.

Mere days after the 2015 Global Climate March, another prominent public space in Paris, the Place du Panthéon, also became inhabited by an action in the interstices between installation and protest: *Ice Watch* by Studio Olafur Eliasson (3–12 December 2015). The name of the installation carried a dual signification: first, the eye we keep on how mass ice surfaces are responding to the continuous warming of the planet, and second, the viewing attitudes we take to our everyday lives as passers-by, observing but not necessarily intervening. *Ice Watch* confronted the civilians and tourists of Paris with the realities of their spectatorship and agency. Through its primary matter, it posed a question as to the implications of tacit acceptance and the margin for turning a blind eye when the crisis facing us is relocated from its remote context to our immediate environment, unnervingly demonstrating, in real time, the fragility of nature and the urgency of calling for action. If deCaires Taylor's art engages with the concept of permanence for its environmental activism, Studio Olafur Eliasson worked on the basis of impermanence, to show that there is no such thing as a resilient natural behemoth that is guaranteed survival. They did so by installing iceberg shapes forming a circle, integrated in the centre of Paris and following the shape of the Place du Panthéon. Inevitably, the structures would exhibit and indeed perform their own disintegration as they began to melt away. As the artists state, the icebergs, 'harvested' from a Greenland fjord, were positioned 'in clock formation' (Eliasson and Rosing). The message was wholly unambiguous: watching comes with consequences, because time is running out.

Beyond such open-space initiatives, we must return to institutional spaces and ask what the theatre can do not only for repertoire but also for operational practices. The route towards sustainable solutions has been explored in the United Kingdom by the Ecovenue project, a partnership between The Theatres Trust and the European Regional Development Fund (ERDF). A three-year project concluding in 2012, Ecovenue involved 48 London performance spaces of different specifications across the city: from the Bush Theatre to the Old Vic, and from TARA Studio to the Duchess Theatre (Stratton 2). Ecovenue is a prime example of how British theatre benefits from European funds. Such funds not only facilitated the project but also positioned it within a broader scale, creating an international paradigm from a world-leading theatre capital with strong potential to inform international practices in artistic organisations and resource management. Whether such essential and ambitious initiatives will continue beyond Brexit, or what funding resources might be in place to support them, remains to be seen.

What Ecovenue set out to accomplish during 2009–2012 was greater transparency and self-reflection as to how theatres are run, the carbon footprint they produce and how any adverse impact on the environment might be offset. Ecovenue framed its remit as interventionist, producing action that was as much urgent for the specific moment in time as it was part of a continuing dialogue and set of endeavours, bequeathing its motivations and methods to future initiatives (Stratton, details provided in different sections of 'Evaluating Ecovenue'). There is, of course, a paradox here, embedded in the very relationship between theatre and environment, as even performances that are driven by the need to generate attention and action against climate change produce their own lingering footprint (a point also made in *2071*). Whether the paradox is inevitable and to what extent this is a necessary side effect of a significant social activity where positives outweigh the negatives, or whether it may be only possible to minimise but never to entirely eliminate the resource consumption that such productions entail, is a question we must keep asking. Still, however, this 'noble' kind of performance remains in the minority. Ecovenue was a timely and important action that logged and highlighted the substantial footprint of London theatres, many of which are not necessarily – or are indeed far from being – committed to environmentally aware repertoire.

In its documentation, Ecovenue engages with a prior initiative, which emphasised the extent of the problem: the Mayor of London's Green Theatre Programme (2008) (Stratton 3–5, 24). In the document emerging from that project, then–London Mayor Boris Johnson recognised that theatre constitutes a major part of London's international image and one of its most considerable income streams (Johnson 4–5). As Johnson stated at the time,

> I am committed to a 60 percent reduction of London's greenhouse gas emissions from 1990 levels by 2025. This plan will help enable all of us to reach that target and avoid some of the potentially disastrous consequences of carrying on 'business as usual'. It will help theatres to communicate the message about climate change to audiences, without imposing on their artistic integrity or reducing the quality of shows. (4)

Considering the support that endeavours like Ecovenue, Green Theatre's successor, have received through the European Union, the task that Johnson sets out becomes considerably more challenging should we reasonably assume that access to such funds might become compromised as a result of Brexit, which was backed by Johnson, among other leading Conservative Party politicians, as part of the 'Leave' campaign in 2016. At the time of the Green Theatre report (September 2008), the London theatre industry carbon footprint was given as 50,000 tonnes a year, with the greatest percentage distribution within that amount being allocated to 'Theatre front of house (day-time and evening, incl. auditorium aircon/cooling)' (*Green Theatre* 8–9), closely followed by the resources required in rehearsal rooms as well as theatre offices. The sample was 136 London theatres (Stratton 3). The equivalent emissions produced by spectators populating these theatres came in at 35,000 tonnes, logged as part of the resources and activity required to physically access the venues (Stratton 3). As part of its findings, the document also provided a comprehensive list of adjustments that could be made towards energy efficiency, including brief references to case studies of theatres that had taken positive steps towards change, and it even offered a 'Carbon calculator for production planning' (*Green Theatre* 32–33).

As far as institutional-level action is concerned in the United Kingdom, since the conclusion of Ecovenue in 2012, no comparable coordinated initiatives have taken place. Summing up the situation in 2015, journalist Holly Williams explored the urgent question of what degree of action is currently being taken, identifying the Arts Council's inclusion of energy efficiency in their selection criteria as a turning point for action at the company level, including, of course, companies of varying sizes and artistic missions. Like Green Theatre, Ecovenue's concluding document also provided practical solutions towards resource efficiency. What both projects shared was a relatively jargon-free lexicon they deployed towards widely communicating the outcomes of the respective endeavours. The major question that such projects raise, however, is what prospects realistically exist towards a long-term commitment to sustainability, individually motivated rather than bound to Arts Council policies. At a time when climate change is given fluctuating attention internationally, the most crucial step for governments claiming an enduring commitment to the environment is the appreciation that raising awareness is not based on isolated acts but requires consistency and depth of time. Only then might claims such as the one Ecovenue makes – that 'it has provided transformative information that will save energy and money in the future' (Stratton 23) – withstand the test of time and deliver actual change, measurable diachronically.

On an international scale, there is some cause for hope. Imagine 2020 (2.0): Art, Ecology & Possible Futures, which began in July 2015, the second phase of Imagine 2020: Art & Climate Change, is a collective effort involving ten European partners, drawing its financial support from the European Union funding scheme Creative Europe. The partners are Artsadmin (the United Kingdom), Bunker (Slovenia), COAL (France), Domino (Croatia), Teatro Maria Matos (Portugal), Kaaitheater (Belgium), Kampnagel (Germany), LIFT (the United Kingdom), Latvijas Jaunā Teātra Institūts (Latvia) and Rotterdamse Schouwburg (the Netherlands). Imagine 2020 defines its mission as 'raising awareness in the cultural field and in a broader civil society context around the issues of the socio-ecological crisis that we are currently facing' ('Imagine 2020'). In order to accomplish this, the project promotes and fosters a wide range of activities converging in the creation and sharing of artistic practices, imperatives and methods that serve to identify and present the key problematics of audiences' and of course the arts sector's relationship to our environment. The significance of Imagine 2020 stems from the fact that its European Union institutional support and reach enable it to establish and foreground the arts as an agent with sustained input that works towards change rather than as a passive field merely responding to funding changes and governmental initiatives, dependent on intermittent financial support. The nature and scale of the environmental crisis is such that it compels artistic collaboration of the magnitude that Imagine 2020 has made possible: outward-facing, intersectional, internationalist. Therefore, once more, the question whether Britain's exit from the European Union might generate a dramatic – and lasting – impact on its participation in EU funding structures that enable work such as Imagine 2020 emerges urgently. Britain's geographical, demographic and symbolic significance in the global political scene, not least in a shifting ground around action against climate change, renders Brexit a considerable factor of indeterminacy as to transnational efforts. The distribution of partners in Imagine 2020 (2.0) is indicative: Britain is the only country to boast two. While it may be encouraging to see that certain artistic organisations in the United Kingdom continue on the path of commitment to sustainability that initiatives such as Ecovenue and Green Theatre have fostered, how such actions may be affected in the years to come through cultural and financial tribulations and adjustments cannot, at this stage, be conclusively determined.

Futures (in Lieu of a Conclusion)

In lieu of a conclusion, this book closes with the challenging yet essential consideration of what the future of eco-theatre and performance might look like. I suggest that theatre scholarship of the future that examines these concerns will need to consider the following: how, if at all, it might be possible to document and account for the impact that environmentally conscious theatre and performance have made in our individual and collective behaviours; how current subsidy structures might enable or hinder the implementation of innovative practices in terms of both subject and sustainability; the difficulties in creating momentum and urgency through theatre in the present moment in such a way that might trigger preventive action for the future without resorting to facile moralising or fear culture; how theatre and performance might negotiate the visual representation of a dystopian future; the offsetting of theatre-making and spectating related carbon footprints and possibilities for sustainable performance; whether environment-focused work runs the risk of an expiration date, given its emphasis on scientific data and how this might be managed; the ethics of our current and future self-performance and community performance as spectators and citizens; a self-reflection regarding the responsibilities of theatre scholarship and potential directions for future discourse, including transitions from traditional historiographies to historicising the present with a view to the future.

As this book closes, I need to revisit the primary directions that theatre scholarship has pursued in relationship to the environmental crisis. What is particularly fascinating is that the field is experiencing encouraging signs of increasing, sustained interest. Indicative sources have already been mentioned, but what is of particular interest to me here is the ambitious interdisciplinary front that is being developed in the work of scholars who are bringing an activist slant to their discourse. Intersections between performance and activism, but also between theatre scholarship and activism, are of course nothing new, but they have mostly concentrated on questions of capitalism, labour and the economy. The environment is a relatively new variable in this landscape, especially in how it is invigorating academic discourses. In this context I particularly wish to note the work of Carl Lavery, whose contribution to the field, like that of Una Chaudhuri and Theresa J. May, is not only expansive but also interventionist and revisionary. By this I mean that Lavery's work produces new ways of reading the familiar text, by introducing the environment as a framing lens, much in the sense that Chaudhuri has called for and that I discuss in the opening pages of this book. Lavery's discourse interrupts our modes of engagement with the canon, disrupting well-trodden methods to produce new models of seeing and interpreting. I selectively mention Lavery's recent work on Samuel Beckett; Eugène Ionesco and the Theatre of the Absurd more broadly; and participative and immersive theatre, or on experiential/autobiographical academic writing.

As Chaudhuri, Lavery, Arons and May's respective work clearly demonstrates, a decisive shift will materialise only once we decidedly interrupt the conversation by adding the environment and ecology (in the broader sense of the word, referring to biorhythms and given spatial contexts and not only to natural preservation) as discourse markers and framing devices rather than as sporadic considerations or accompaniments. Similarly, it does not suffice, when we think and write of theatre and the environment, to reflect on only case studies of works that specifically deal with climate change and related concerns. Rather, we need to return to the canon, revisit, reread and revise. May offers a directly applicable model for how this may be achieved in the shape of a series of questions that prioritise the environment and that can be asked of any play or, I would also note, performance. She calls this 'Some Green Questions to Ask a Play' ('Beyond Bambi' 105). Such a method, if it takes hold, will not only deepen our understanding of a given text and/or performance piece but also create new ground for novel analyses of theatre that might occasionally be thought of as familiar, overwritten about or even safe. As environmentally driven scholarship stands to reveal, questions pertaining to ecologies are never safe, and they can always upset and disrupt the common ground of what a text or performance stands for if we dedicate space and time to them in a sustained and systematic way.

When we talk of the theatre, we can ignore neither the spectator, a point that Helen Freshwater made in one of the seminal early contributions to this series, *Theatre & Audience*, nor the environment and landscape – again, in the broadest sense (backdrop; set; spatial location/venue; social, political, historical and natural conditions) – of a text or performance piece. Our interpretative and interventionist capabilities as spectators, citizens and agents for a cultural and political shift ought always to be informed by how we interact with, protect and generally account for our environment. This covers everything from our viewing and consumption habits on our way to and in the theatre to how we might take forward the ideas put across in a given show in a way that prompts us to further consider our responsibilities to nature. As is widely acknowledged, our experience of how we interact with and interpret performance does not begin in the space of the show, but rather, it is shaped by our encounters, habits, triggers and, generally, the moments and events well before it. This is because our civic agency is always with us, a part of our everyday lives and therefore cannot be switched off as extrinsic to our experience as spectators. The same, as Lavery notes, applies to creating and devising processes for new performance ('Introduction'). To broaden this further, if we accept that life can be categorised into and analysed as a series of events and performances of different kinds, much in the way that Richard Schechner has outlined, we also need to revisit such theories of performance and inject the environment as a factor weighing upon those discourses. Again, a historical, social, political and cultural context can no longer be discussed without the primary consideration of the environment. To do so, as scholars, citizens, spectators and individuals, would be irresponsible – especially in our given moment of dire environmental crisis. The environment, therefore, is not an additional factor or a laborious parameter but instead an intrinsic tone setter and an always already present concern, indeed primary to others. Meanwhile, as work concerning climate justice and Indigenous populations continues to flourish in theatre practice and scholarship, environmentalism finds a natural partner in postcolonialism, both offering assessments of the present and taking stock of transgressive pasts: the big Cs of consumption and colonialism. In the coming years, it will be crucial to see how this field develops into its own right.

The remit of this book has been particular in that it takes shape within a relatively limited space and must from the onset prioritise case studies that will cover a wide and broad enough spectrum to be representative but that, at the same time, will speak to each other in a way that enables a critical perspective to take shape. A book of the specific length cannot be, nor should it claim to be, exhaustive. It forms part of a developing conversation, and the more accounts of environmentally driven performances that we can commit to paper, the better the contribution we will make to scholarship and to general readership. As a theatre theorist and historian based in the Western world, I am concerned with tracing the legacies of transgression, exploitation and privilege that have produced our present crisis, a topic that I continue to explore in different aspects of my work (see, for example, my book *Social and Political Theatre in 21st-Century Britain: Staging Crisis*, which also responds to the question of the environment and economics). I am equally invested in accounting for the possibilities and modes of positive present intervention. Our current historical moment is indeed pivotal: for the legacies it will bequeath to future generations and for the civic frustration and discontent with recent political developments whose outcome on international policies of collaboration across different fields remains uncertain. As May observes, 'We live in a watershed moment––in all senses of that phrase' ('Beyond Bambi' 96). The book is of its moment in time, although I hope it might become a tool for future historiographies. Its aim, therefore, has been to account for significant examples that fall within its parameters of enquiry and indeed, where possible, for instances that have not been dealt with extensively in prior publications. It is not possible for this book, because of its scope, to fully take on the revisionist mission that I and other colleagues call for as essential, because it has had to focus specifically on work that revolves around the environment as a thematic concern and, in many ways, as producing, staging and/or installing principle and guide. I hope that the reader will draw on this book in ways that will facilitate their own engagement with these concerns. In future publications, I look forward to specifically engaging with the revisionist approach to the canon through the lens of the environment.

May offers a powerful articulation for some of the dilemmas that continue to permeate discourses: 'Does ecocriticism seem placid, too contemplative, or even indulgent in the face of present day horrors? … In this vein, a colleague once chided me for my so-called tree-hugging "Bambi-esque" interests' ('Beyond Bambi' 96). Here, then, is the conundrum: How do we break through? How do we activate, disrupt and move away from the human as defining measure? May concludes that

> At a time when so many longstanding human endeavors seem to have endangered the integrity

> of all earth's species, ecocriticism can expose and dismantle the ideologies and master narratives that shore up business as usual and inspire performances that help society recalibrate toward sustainable human means. ('Beyond Bambi' 104)

In a recent essay, Chaudhuri writes that 'the term Anthropocene performs a conceptual feat: it designates a single species – ours – as a geophysical force' ('Anthropo-Scenes' 305). Chaudhuri concludes that 'The ecological crisis of our time – resulting as it partly does from a history of bad ideas and broken thinking – demands that we think and rethink the terms of belonging, for our species and others, on this planet' (309). Chaudhuri's position creates a fruitful dialogue that Lavery's research is also seminal to. By asking 'What Can Theatre Do?', Lavery offers a pragmatic assessment of the scholarly field and the trends that have shaped its exchanges, avoiding a critical voice of doom while also steering clear of proclamations about a by-default catalytic power of performance when it comes to these difficult issues and the questions that arise from them. Lavery, in a way that allows for affinities with Chaudhuri's discourse, frames his work by noting that 'Without ever wanting to collapse the very real distance between theatrical acts and real ones, theatre's mode of doing was posited as a unique form of praxis, … [which] might have the capacity to alter how we exist in the world by troubling conventional modes of thinking and feeling' ('Introduction' 229–230). Therefore, we must recognise that in performance and no less performance that deals with ecology, there is also value in acknowledging 'weakness and inadequacy' ('Introduction' 233). This subtracts from neither the case study nor its analysis. Rather, it preserves both from grandiose claims that do not necessarily – or it is difficult to prove otherwise – correspond to reality and result. If we are to speak of interventionist theatre scholarship regarding drama, performance and the environment, such are the methods that we need to pursue going forward: we need to be taking stock, asking these questions and working towards producing our part of the solution in future publications and discourses. And we need to do this while recognising, and having it recognised in other disciplines, that a singularly focused approach driven by one specific scholarly field towards a problem so multifaceted is fraught with difficulties. On the contrary, opening up to multiple channels of communication, collaboration and exchange with disciplines beyond our own, on terms as equal as possible, is essential.

bibliography

2071. Royal Court Theatre, n. d., http://www.royalcourttheatre.com/

Abrahams, Guy, Fiona Armstrong and Deborah Hart. *Climarte: Arts for a Safer Climate*. 2010–2016, www.climarte.org.

Abrahams, Guy, and Bronwyn Johnson. *ART+CLIMATE=CHANGE*, 2017, www.artclimatechange.org.

'Alt om Henrik Ibsen.' *Nasjonalbiblioteket*, 2017, web.archive.org/web/20170630093245/http://ibsen.nb.no/id/1998.0

Angelaki, Vicky. *Social and Political Theatre in 21st-Century Britain: Staging Crisis*. Bloomsbury, 2017.

Arons, Wendy, and Theresa J. May, eds. *Readings in Performance and Ecology*. Palgrave Macmillan, 2012.

ARTCOP21. n. d., www.artcop21.com.

Bartlett, Mike. *Earthquakes in London*. Methuen, 2010.

Beitiks, Meghan Moe, Ian Garrett and Miranda Wright, eds. *On Environment. CSPA Quarterly*, vol. 12, 2015.

Billington, Michael. '2071 Five-star Review – Urgent Call for the Greatest Collective Action in History.' *Guardian*, 7 November 2014, www.theguardian.com/stage/2014/nov/07/2071-review-urgent-call-history-royal-court-theatre

Bilodeau, Chantal. 'As the Climate Change Threat Grows, So Does a Theatrical Response.' *American Theatre*, 2016, https://www.americantheatre.org/2016/03/30/as-the-climate-change-threat-grows-so-does-a-theatrical-response/

Bilodeau, Chantal, et al. *Artists and Climate Change*. n. d., www.artistsandclimatechange.com

Bottoms, Stephen, Aaron Franks and Paula Kramer, eds. *On Ecology*. *Performance Research*, vol. 17, no. 4, 2012.

Bottoms, Stephen, and Matthew Goulish, eds. *Small Acts of Repair: Performance, Ecology and Goat Island*. Routledge, 2017.

Carrington, Damian. 'The Anthropocene Epoch: Scientists Declare Dawn of Human-Influenced Age.' *Guardian*, 29 August 2016, www.theguardian.com/environment/2016/aug/29/declare-anthropocene-epoch-experts-urge-geological-congress-human-impact-earth

Chaudhuri, Una. 'Anthropo-Scenes: Staging Climate Chaos in the Drama of Bad Ideas.' *Twenty-First Century Drama: What Happens Now*, edited by Siân Adiseshiah and Louise LePage, Palgrave Macmillan, 2016, pp. 303–321.

———. 'Climate Lens: Birth of a Post-Nation!' *HowlRound Theatre Commons*, 2017, www.howlround.com/climate-lens-birth-of-a-post-nation/

Christopher, Karen, et al. 'It's an Earthquake in My Heart'. *Goat Island Performance*, n. d., http://www.goatislandperformance.org/perf_earthquake.htm

———. 'It's Shifting, Hank.' *Goat Island Performance*, n. d., www.goatislandperformance.org/perf_shiftinghank.htm

———. 'The Sea and Poison.' *Goat Island Performance*, n. d., http://www.goatislandperformance.org/perf_SnP.htm

———. 'When Will the September Roses Bloom? Last Night Was Only a Comedy: A Double Performance.' *Goat Island Performance*, n. d., http://www.goatislandperformance.org/perf_septemberRoses.htm

Churchill, Caryl. *Escaped Alone*. Nick Hern Books, 2016.

———. *Far Away*. Nick Hern Books, 2000.

———. *Not Not Not Not Not Enough Oxygen*. *Caryl Churchill: Shorts*. Nick Hern Books, 1990.

Cless, Downing. *Ecology and Environment in European Drama*. Routledge, 2010.

'Climate Change Theatre Action 2017 Edition.' *The Arctic Cycle*, 2017, https://www.thearcticcycle.org/ccta-2017/

DeCaires Taylor, Jason. 'Colonised.' *Underwater Sculpture*, n. d., www.underwatersculpture.com/environment/environment-threats.

———. 'Threats.' *Underwatersculpture*, n. d., www.underwatersculpture.com/environment/environment-threats

'Eco-, Comb. Form.' *Oxford English Dictionary*, http://www.oed.com. Access provided by the University of Reading, n. d.

Eliasson, Olafur, and Minik Rosing. *Ice Watch Paris*, n. d., www.icewatchparis.com

Emmott, Stephen. *Ten Billion*. Penguin, 2013.

'Far Away.' *Corcadorca*, 2018, http://www.corcadorca.com/website/far-away/

Freshwater, Helen. *Theatre & Audience*. Red Globe Press, 2009.

Giannachi, Gabriella, and Nigel Stewart, eds. *Performing Nature: Explorations in Ecology and the Arts*. Peter Lang, 2006.

'Global Climate March.' *350*, n. d., www.350.org/global-climate-march

Green Theatre: Taking Action on Climate Change, 2008, www.london.gov.uk/sites/default/files/green_theatre_summary.pdf/

Grindstaff, Jessica, and Erik Sanko. 'About.' *Phantom Limb Company*, n. d., www.phantomlimbcompany.com/about/

———. 'Falling Out.' *Phantom Limb Company*, n. d., http://phantomlimbcompany.com/fallingout/

———. 'Memory Rings.' *Phantom Limb Company*, n. d., http://phantomlimbcompany.com/memoryrings/

———. '69°S.' *Phantom Limb Company*, n. d., http://phantomlimbcompany.com/69south/

Grode, Eric. 'Tale of Antarctic Explorers, Lives Hanging by a Thread.' *The New York Times*, 3 Nov. 2011, www.nytimes.com/2011/11/04/theater/reviews/69s-at-bam-harvey-theater-review.html/

Heddon, Dee, and Sally Mackey, eds. *Themed Edition: Environmentalism. Research in Drama Education: The Journal of Applied Theatre and Performance*, vol. 17, no. 2, 2012.

Hickson, Ella. *Oil*. Nick Hern Books, 2016.

Ibsen, Henrik. *Ein Volksfeind*, 23 December 2017, Burgtheater, Vienna. Performance.

Imagine 2020: Art and Climate Change. n. d., http://www.imagine2020.eu

Isherwood, Charles. 'Review: "Memory Rings." Forget about It.' *The New York Times*, 18 November 2016, www.nytimes.com/2016/11/19/theater/review-memory-rings-forget-about-it.html/

Johnson, Boris. 'Foreword.' *Green Theatre: Taking Action on Climate Change*, 2008, www.london.gov.uk/sites/default/files/green_theatre_summary.pdf/

Kelleher, Olivia. 'Burial of Graves at Spike Island "hid evidence" of Mass Deaths.' *The Irish Times*, 22 May 2016, www.irishtimes.com/news/crime-and-law/burial-of-graves-at-spike-island-hid-evidence-of-mass-deaths-1.2656637

Kershaw, Baz. *Theatre Ecology: Environments and Performance Events*. Cambridge University Press, 2007.

Köck, Thomas. *Klimatrilogie: paradies fluten / paradies hungern / paradies spielen*. Suhrkamp Verlag, 2017.

———. *paradies fluten*. 9 Sept. 2017, Akademietheater, Vienna. Performance.

Lavery, Carl. 'Ecology in Beckett's Theatre Garden: Or How to Cultivate the Oikos.' *Contemporary Theatre Review*, vol. 28, no. 1, pp. 10–26.

———. 'Introduction: Performance and Ecology – What Can Theatre Do?' *Performance and Ecology: What Can Theatre Do?. Green Letters: Studies in Ecocriticism*, vol. 20, no. 3, 2016, pp. 229–236.

———. 'Part 1: Carl Lavery.' *Walking, Writing and Performance: Autobiographical Texts by Deirdre Heddon, Carl Lavery, Phil Smith*, edited by Roberta Mock, Intellect Books, 2009, pp. 25–56.

———. 'Participation, Ecology, Cosmos.' *Reframing Immersive Theatre: The Politics and Pragmatics of Participatory Performance*, edited by James Frieze, Palgrave Macmillan, 2016, pp. 301–315.

Lavery, Carl, ed. *Performance and Ecology: What Can Theatre Do? Green Letters: Studies in Ecocriticism*, vol. 20, no. 3, 2016.

Lavery, Carl, and Clare Finburgh, eds. *Rethinking the Theatre of the Absurd: Ecology, the Environment and the Greening of the Modern Stage*. Bloomsbury, 2015.

Lonergan, Patrick. 'Caryl Churchill's Theatre of the Antropocene: *Far Away* by Corcadorca.' *Scenes from the Bigger Picture*, 17 June 2017, www.patricklonergan.wordpress.com/2017/06/17/caryl-churchills-theatre-of-the-antropocene-far-away-by-corcadorca/

Macmillan, Duncan. *Lungs*. Oberon, 2011.

Macmillan, Duncan, and Chris Rapley. *2071*. *Royal Court Theatre*, n. d., www.royalcourttheatre.com/

Macmillan, Duncan, Katie Mitchell, Chris Rapley and Christopher Campbell. '2071 at The Royal Court Theatre.' *Royal Court Theatre*, 5 November 2014, www.royalcourttheatre.com/news/podcasts/2071-podcast/

May, Theresa J. 'Beyond Bambi: Towards a Dangerous Ecocriticism in Theatre Studies.' *Theatre Topics*, vol. 17, no. 2, 2007.

McKie, Robin. 'Royal Court Play 2071 Will Look into Future of Humankind after Global Warming.' *Guardian*, 1 November 2014, https://www.theguardian.com/environment/2014/nov/01/royal-court-play-2071-global-warming/

———. 'Stephen Emmott: Overpopulation Is at the Root of All the Planet's Troubles.' *Guardian*, 15 July 2012, https://www.theguardian.com/technology/2012/jul/15/overpopulation-root-planet-problems-emmott/

McNulty, Charles. 'Inspired, Enchanting Puppet Theater with a Punch: The Eco-themed "Memory Rings."' *Los Angeles Times*, 9 April 2016, http://www.latimes.com/entertainment/arts/culture/la-et-cm-memory-rings-review-20160409-column.html/

Merritt, Stephanie. 'Climate Change Play 2071 Aims to Make Data Dramatic.' *Guardian*, 5 November 2014, www.theguardian.com/stage/2014/nov/05/climate-change-theatre-2071-katie-mitchell-duncan-macmillan/

Mitchell, Katie. 'I'm Fighting to save Night Trains – the Ticket to My Daughter's Future.' *Guardian*, 18 September 2014, https://www.theguardian.com/commentisfree/2014/sep/18/save-night-trains-ticket-daughter-rail-greenest-travel-europe-sleeper-services/

No Passport. n. d., www.nopassport.org/

Oltermann, Philip. 'End of the Line for Europe's Iconic Night Trains?' *Guardian*, 12 September 2014, www.theguardian.com/world/2014/sep/12/europe-night-trains-sleeper-service/

O'Riordan, Sean. 'Spike Island Prison Riot Exhibition Opens 30 Years After "mob rule just took over."' *Irish Examiner*, 2 September 2015, https://www.irishexaminer.com/ireland/spike-island-prison-riot-exhibition-opens-30-years-after-mob-rule-just-took-over-351455.html/

Peltier, Elian. 'With Marches Banned, Shoes Carry a Message.' *The New York Times,* 29 November 2015, www.nytimes.com/interactive/projects/cp/climate/2015-paris-climate-talks/

Perrier, Jean-François. 'Entretien avec Katie Mitchell et Stephen Emmott.' *Festival Avignon*, n. d., www.festival-avignon.com/

Petsch, Barbara. 'Jette Steckel: Ibsen und die Ökologie.' *Die Presse*, 15 November 2017, www.diepresse.com/home/kultur/news/5317158/Jette-Steckel_Ibsen-und-die-Oekologie/

Phantom Limb: 69°S. Created by Jessica Grindstaff and Erik Sanko, directed by Sophie Hunter, EMPAC, 2011, *Vimeo*.

Rapley, Chris, and Duncan Macmillan. 'Climate Change Is Not Just about Science – It's about the Future We Want to Create.' *Guardian*, 22 November 2014, https://www.theguardian.com/science/2014/nov/22/-sp-climate-change-special-report/

Roseingrave, Louise. 'Hopes for Alcatraz-style Tourism after Handover of Cork's Spike Island.' *Irish Times*, 29 July 2009, https://www.irishtimes.com/news/hopes-for-alcatraz-style-tourism-after-handover-of-cork-s-spike-island-1.708457/

Schechner, Richard. *Performance Studies: An Introduction*. Routledge, 2002.

The Shackleton Project/69 Degrees. Created by Jessica Grindstaff and Erik Sanko, directed by Sophie Hunter, Brooklyn Academy of Music, 2011–2012, *YouTube*.

69°S (The Shackleton Project). Created by Jessica Grindstaff and Erik Sanko, directed by Sophie Hunter, EMPAC, 2011, *Vimeo*.

Slovic, Scott, ed. *ISLE: Interdisciplinary Studies in Literature and Environment*. Oxford University Press.

Stephens, Simon. *Wastwater*. Methuen Drama, 2011.

Stratton, Craig, et al. 'Evaluating Ecovenue.' *The Theatres Trust*, n. d., www.theatrestrust.org.uk/store/assets/0000/2960/Evaluating_Ecovenue.pdf/

Szerszynski, Bronislaw, Wallace Heim and Claire Waterton, eds. *Nature Performed: Environment, Culture and Performance*. Blackwell, 2003.

Welt-Klimakonferenz (World Climate Change Conference). Created by Helgard Haug, Stefan Kaegi and Daniel Wetzel, Deutsches Schauspielhaus Hamburg, 2014, *Vimeo*.

Williams, Holly. 'British Theatres Going Green as Venues across the Land Do Their Bit to Reduce Carbon Emissions.' *Independent*, 4 October 2015, http://www.independent.co.uk/environment/

british-theatres-going-green-as-venues-across-the-land-do-their-bit-to-reduce-carbon-emissions-a6678941.html

Wimmer, Helmut, and Karlheinz Essl. *The Last Day*. 2018, Kunsthistorisches Museum, Vienna.

Zalasiewicz, Jan, et al. 'When Did the Anthropocene Begin? A Mid-twentieth Century Boundary Level Is Stratigraphically Optimal.' *Quaternary International*, no. 373, 2015, pp. 196–203.

index

acknowledgements

I thank sincerely the academic colleagues who have invited me to present research in the context of this book. I must also thank the University of Reading for awarding me a 2020 Research Fellowship in relation to this project.

I am grateful for the generosity with which Professor Ian Fairchild contributed to my conference at the University of Birmingham in 2016 on the environment, the economy and climate change. Although this book was written after that time, I had no doubt that Ian would be the ideal person to write the foreword, and I thank him for the exemplary openness with which he embraces the prospect for more substantial exchange between the arts and sciences. Ian's performance work *Introducing the Anthropocene* embodies this very ideal.

My warmest thanks go to Jen Harvie and Dan Rebellato, to Sonya Barker, Emily Lovelock and Nicola Cattini, as well as to the anonymous colleague who peer-reviewed my manuscript. I am grateful for all your support.

I am also grateful to my publisher's creative team, who imagined the cover art for this book. It captures all that I might have hoped for.

Vicky Angelaki